SACRED SEED

THE GOLDEN SUFI CENTER® PUBLISHING

"The way we live and act is determined by the perceptual lenses that are shaped by our beliefs and values. Our belief that it is our right to use as we wish, any part of the biosphere—air, water, soil, other life-forms—has created problem after problem. If life is sacred, then we cannot treat other organisms as if they are cars or computers, we must act with humility, respect, and love. This book provides a powerful perspective to temper our unseemly rush to engineer everything within the biosphere."

—**David Suzuki**, author, *The Sacred Balance*

"There is no more beautiful gift from nature than the seed—and its protection is vital to our survival. Vandana Shiva, Navdanya, the Global Peace Initiative of Women, and the brilliant spiritual leaders who contributed their voices to this book are all elevating our dialogue about seeds, and the profound role they hold for the future of all humankind."

—**Alice Waters**, chef, author, and culinary visionary

"These essays establish, with clarity and eloquence, a single crucial insight: our spiritual well-being and our approach to the use of the Earth for our nourishment are inseparable. We have woken up to the fact that the problem of food security is painfully pressing for the coming generation: what this book tells us is that we cannot address this without thinking again very radically about how we see our human growth and nurture; and we cannot cultivate a 'spirituality' that pays no attention to the facts of hunger, waste, environmental degradation, and so on. This is an exceptional testimony to the holistic thinking our society so desperately needs."

—**Dr. Rowan Williams**, former Archbishop of Canterbury, and current Master of Magdalene College, Cambridge

"A reverence for our ancient seeds is essential to our very survival. *Sacred Seed* explains in beautiful detail how and why we must protect them."

—**Ed Begley, Jr.**, American actor, director, and environmentalist

"This book is timely and timeless in its importance. The seeds that bring forth life and food for our planet and its people are indispensable for the continuity of all living things. Thus our care for seeds is one of the most vital things we can do amid our many challenges of the present. These articles light a luminous path forward."

—**Mary Evelyn Tucker**, co-director, Forum on Religion and Ecology at Yale University

"Ever since I watched the women in Bangladeshi farm families carefully saving seed from one generation to the next, I've pondered on this greatest symbol of our connection through time to those who came before and those who will come after. This book is a rich storehouse of wisdom for all the springs to come."

—**Bill McKibben**, founder, 350.org

"Through the seeds, they say, speak the voices of the ancestors. It's hard to imagine a more timely moment than now—when the global biodiversity of seeds is so dangerously under threat, and with the hopefulness and promise that seeds symbolize and embody—for this gathering of sacred voices to emerge. Gift yourself with the vitality of this collection, and share it, to revitalize your community and encourage restoring a sense of sacredness to our foods, and health, and security."

—**Nina Simons**, president and co-founder, Bioneers, and past president, Seeds of Change

"Caring for seeds is caring for one of the most evolutionarily profound and numinous expressions of life. At this critical time in human history, seeds could not be more important, and this beautiful and transformative book, *Sacred Seed*, is an exquisite poetic testimony that reconnects us to the very web of life. Each author offers elegant wisdom and heartfelt praise of life-giving seeds."

—**Osprey Orielle Lake**, founder, Women's Earth and Climate Caucus

"*Sacred Seed* is not only a homage to the endangered nourishment of our planet but to the spiritual source of our lives. Each reading is both a teaching and a prayer, and the beauty of the illustrations alone is enough to make me want to keep this book by my bed or next to my meditation pillow for years, there to provide inspiration when I need it. Drawing from diverse sources, it feeds our longing for the sacred while it awakens the energy to act so that our grandchildren and theirs will enjoy strong, healthy, and sacred lives."

—**Mirabai Bush**, senior fellow and associate director, The Center for Contemplative Mind in Society

"Through gorgeous photography and essays spanning many traditions, this book offers a diversity of lenses to view the sacredness of seed."

—**Charles Eisenstein**, author and speaker

"'How many are your works, Lord! . . . The earth is full of your creatures . . . teeming with creatures beyond number. . . . May the glory of the Lord endure forever . . .' (Psalms 104). Whether secular or religious, we must recognize and preserve the bounty of nature or we stand to lose our very humanity."

—**James Hansen**, former director, NASA Goddard Institute for Space Studies, and current director of Climate Science, Awareness and Solutions Program at Columbia University Earth Institute

"Preserving seed diversity—our vast and beautiful heritage of seeds—is one of the most pressing crises facing the human community. Our future depends on our courageous actions now. May these essays by great spiritual voices from around the world awaken us to value, care for, and stand up for the seeds that nature has gifted to us."

—**Frances Moore Lappé**, author, *Diet for a Small Planet* and *EcoMind*

"To name a seed as *sacred* is to make a small but emphatic protest against its commodification, genetic manipulation, and corporate control. But such naming does more; it moves us beyond protest and calls forth a necessary reverence for the material stuff of Creation. In this fine collection of essays the subject is seeds, but what these authors call for is nothing less than the re-enchantment of the world."

—**Fred Bahnson**, author, *Soil and Sacrament: A Spiritual Memoir of Food and Faith,* and director of Food, Faith, and Religious Leadership Initiative at Wake Forest University School of Divinity

"This rich and much needed collection of essays inspired in me my own prayer, The Prayer of the Seed: 'I am but small and seemingly insignificant yet I bear life in my tiny body. I am a source of hope for a hungry and hurting world. So I pray, treasure me as precious—source of life for God's creatures.'"

—**Rev. Dr. Joan Brown Campbell**, chair, Global Peace Initiative of Women, and former general secretary, National Council of the Churches of Christ

"This book, its very theme, and its reverent illustrations have the taste and scent of holiness! The humble seed on which we totally depend is just as invisible, humble, and unappreciated as holiness itself often is. As a Franciscan, I know that is exactly where we find the greatest mystery and the most alluring truth."

—**Fr. Richard Rohr**, O.F.M., Center for Action and Contemplation, Albuquerque, New Mexico

"... a testament to the relevance of the seed selection of our ancestors that we have an obligation to continue for ourselves and future generations; seed saving, and by extension appropriate selection, is a natural behaviour of humankind and a very important part of our positive position in the potentially infinite cycle of life on Earth. Without governing ethics, science has continued in a direction of seed manipulation that can only be honestly described as sociopathic behaviour governed only by short-term greed."

—**Geoff Lawton**, world-renowned permaculture designer and teacher, www.geofflawton.com

"... The present unspeakable violence to seeds, which is a human-caused tragedy, has too often been tacitly condoned through silence. In no small way the perspectives of an evolving universe have catalyzed the writings in this book, and they counteract that silence with an expansion of the rich spiritual legacy of traditional wisdoms. We need these words now more than ever ..."

—**Miriam MacGillis**, O.P., director, Genesis Farm

"By virtue of the fact that 'the end is in the beginning' with reference to everything in life, the primordial sacredness of a 'seed' is a reality we should all embrace. This brilliant series of essays by the most distinguished of spiritual thinkers reveals every aspect of this truth with great force and clarity. All thanks go to those who have compiled this remarkable offering."

—**John Reed**, author, *Elegant Simplicity*

"Generative inspiration and awakening thoughts pour out of these pages like seeds waiting to land in the rich soil of cultivated empathy. Tend them with the light of thinking and the warmth of interest, and invite the miraculous to emerge."

—**Martin Ping**, executive director,
Hawthorne Valley Association

"Ancient cultures representing the world's wisdom traditions maintained a sacred connection to seeds and agriculture; evolving with the natural world as one. As humanity becomes more and more disconnected from the natural world, so do our relationships with the life-supporting systems that we are destroying faster than our ability to understand the future consequences and impacts. Extinction of traditional seed species is likely to be one of our longest-lasting legacies and likely our own extinction. The essays in *Sacred Seed* present us with another possibility, an urgent awakening and honoring that reunites seeds with the sacred."

—**Suzanne Marstrand**, founder, Earth Origin Seeds,
www.manitou.org

"Seed is life. *Sacred Seed* brings to light that we are killing ourselves by destroying the very seed of life . . . the gift of God, the word of God. . . . A first of its kind, this collection of articles from great spiritual and cultural leaders from around the world reflects the cosmic intelligence embedded in all forms of life, where seed acts as the source and the connection to the higher self. Seed is a part of natural law and a fight against it is not only unlawful but harmful to our coexistence in the true sense. . . . I recommend to all people on our planet to understand deeply the implications of GMOs in light of the significance, meaning, and power of seed. An indigenous seed can bring the Earth back to life."

—**Dr. Saamdu Chetri**, executive director,
GNH (Gross National Happiness) Center, Bhutan

"Almost 100 years ago, Liberty Hyde Bailey admonished us to adopt a 'new hold' with respect to agriculture and our entire relationship with nature, a 'hold' that recognized the importance 'for spiritual contact.' Such a 'new hold' constitutes a cultural transformation that is essential to the survival of the human species. *Sacred Seed* is an inspiring collection of brief essays, from a variety of faith communities, that can help inspire us to engage this important transformation."

—**Frederick Kirschenmann**, author, *Cultivating an Ecological Conscience: Essays from a Farmer Philosopher*

"Seeds are *it*, containing within their humble abode all of life's potency, promise, and potential. This beauteous book is a call to conscious action. It is chock full of seeds ready to take root in hearts and minds, sparking a reverentially infectious connection to life's sacred beginnings."

—**Trathen Heckman**, director, Daily Acts, and board president, Transition US

"Here is a beautiful mandala of voices of religious leaders worldwide, bringing moral imperative to the fight for seeds. Human salvation depends on seed salvation. I devoured the teachings of this holy text—seeds as the bridge over death, seeds as compassion. . ."

—**Janisse Ray**, author, *The Seed Underground: A Growing Revolution to Save Seeds*

"*Sacred Seed* honors farmers and eaters around the world who recognize that seeds are not only the foundation of the food system, but that their preservation is intricately tied to the preservation of humanity. Seeds provide both dietary and cultural diversity—reminding us of our past and providing us with future sustenance. The essays in this book show us the true value of protecting seeds for both present and future generations—and that the time to take action is now!"

—**Danielle Nierenberg**, president, Food Tank:
The Food Think Tank, www.foodtank.com

"This collection of short meditations leads to the image of the seed as a spiritual potency that mediates transformation and life on Earth. A sense of respect, a desire to care, and the will to protect grows in the soul when we begin to recognize this potency. It is this transformation of our inner relation to the world that provides deep and sustaining ground for environmental awareness and activism. That is a central message of the book. The authors of the meditations are rooted in different spiritual traditions and many of them are also activists. Moving through the variety of perspectives I could sense a common ground of insight and concern that informs the traditions—a unity that is all the more potent when spoken through the diverse voices."

—**Craig Holdrege**, PhD, director,
The Nature Institute

SACRED SEED

Introduction by Dr. Vandana Shiva

Essays by:

His All Holiness Ecumenical Patriarch Bartholomew
Pir Zia Inayat-Khan · His Holiness the 17th Gyalwang Karmapa, Ogyen Trinley Dorje
Sister Joan Chittister, OSB · Llewellyn Vaughan-Lee · Chief Tamale Bwoya
Swami Veda Bharati · Tiokasin Ghosthorse · Rabbi Arthur Waskow
Blu Greenberg & others

THE GOLDEN SUFI CENTER® PUBLISHING

First published in the United States in 2014 by
The Golden Sufi Center
P.O. Box 456, Point Reyes, California 94956
www.goldensufi.org

ISBN: 978-1-890350-63-5

Library of Congress Cataloging-in-Publication Data available upon request.

Cover photograph by Ana Castilho: www.facebook.com/Mandalanas.
Printed in China by Global Interprint, Santa Rosa, California.

TABLE OF CONTENTS

DEDICATION

To all those working to preserve and care for the Earth
and Her life systems.

ACKNOWLEDGMENTS

This book was inspired by the impassioned efforts for ecological preservation and love of the Earth of each contributor, and the leadership and vision of Dr. Vandana Shiva and the Navdanya community. We are thankful to Dena Merriam for setting the thematic context of this timely collection. Gratitude goes to Ross and Hildur Jackson of the Gaia Foundation for their early support of this project. We also wish to acknowledge Susan Slack for her editorial direction and the photographic contributions of Ana Castilho, Kartikey Shiva, Henriette Kress, Lisa Kleger, Deana Holbova, and others. We are also grateful to our young leader and graphic designer in Kashmir, Mudasir Kubrawi, Anat Vaughan-Lee, and graphic designer Kamilla Talbot for the book's design and layout. Remembering that work with seeds belongs to the feminine mysteries of the Earth and the soul, we are grateful to the Global Peace Initiative of Women, to Marianne Marstrand and Janelle Surpris, for their careful tending of *Sacred Seed* so that it could be brought into the light.

FOREWORD

For more than ten years the Global Peace Initiative of Women has been fostering peacebuilding activities in many troubled regions of the world. Through these efforts we have come to realize that the most dangerous war humankind is engaged in is the war against nature, the often unrecognized or unacknowledged violence we are perpetrating against the natural world. Human violence and violence against nature are directly linked. Until we can learn to live peacefully and respectfully with Earth's community of life, we will not live peacefully with each other. In other words, for us to create a more peaceful world, we must change the way we relate to the whole of the natural world.

Among the most serious of these acts of violence against nature is the destruction of the sacred seed. Thus we decided to gather spiritual voices to show that the destruction of natural seeds is a spiritual matter, not merely an economic, political, or agricultural issue. There are profound spiritual implications to what we are doing to our seeds, which are, after all, the very source of our survival.

The seed is among the most sacred gifts of nature, and yet in modern times we have come to take this gift very much for granted. Nature has provided a tremendous variety of crops to give us all the nutrients we need for a healthy life. As humankind developed the technology to manipulate the seed, so too did this diversity begin to diminish, to our own detriment. Over the last decades we have lost most of our seed and crop diversity, and this loss directly impacts human health.

Science is also a gift of nature, and if used wisely can enhance human life. Too often, however, humankind develops technologies without applying the wisdom to use these advances to our true benefit—meaning long-term well-being. As a human community we look to short-term fixes without considering long-term impacts. Profit also overrides community and ecological well-being. Perhaps the most dangerous of our technological advances in recent times is the ability to take away the reproductive capability from seeds—to create suicide seeds that do not reproduce themselves. Seeds are living entities and to take away their reproductive power is to kill their life energy—to destroy their life-giving properties, which help to nourish us. Technology without wisdom is deadly. Clearly humankind must develop the wisdom to understand the spiritual dimensions of the technologies being developed. There is an urgency to respond to the seed crisis. That is why we have decided to produce this book in partnership with Navdanya. Our hope is that the Seed Freedom Campaign initiated by Dr. Vandana Shiva will be adopted by spiritual communities around the world.

There is an important role to be played by spiritual leaders and practitioners—those who have the wisdom and compassion to understand the breadth of the agricultural and ecological crises we are needlessly creating. To manipulate nature's life energies is to directly harm Earth's ecological systems and human health. Hopefully the human community will pause, reflect, and learn to treasure again the sacred gift of the natural seed, which when used wisely can provide for all the needs of the growing human family.

Dena Merriam
Founder and Convener, Global Peace Initiative of Women

INTRODUCTION

Vandana Shiva

For the past four decades I have dedicated my life to the defense of biodiversity, and the integrity and well-being of all species, including all humans. For the past three decades I have been working in the service of seed freedom, and through it contributing to Earth Democracy for the well-being of all.

I started Navdanya, a network of seed keepers and organic producers, in 1987 when I first heard corporations speak of their plans to genetically modify every seed, patent seeds, and impose patents on life laws, globally. A patent is granted for an invention. Patents on seed transform our highest sacred duties of sharing and saving seed into "intellectual property crimes."

I am inspired by the sanctity of life, the sacredness of seed. How can corporations claim to be the creators and inventors of life on Earth when all they have the capacity of doing is to introduce toxic genes into the cells of plants by means of gene guns and plant cancers?

Navdanya means "nine seeds" (symbolizing protection of biological and cultural diversity). Navdanya also means "new gift." We see our work as reclaiming the gift of the commons, of saving and sharing seeds.

Whatever happens to seed affects the web of life.

When seed is living and regenerative and diverse, it feeds the pollinators, the soil organisms, and the animals, including humans.

When seed is non-renewable, bred for chemicals, or genetically engineered with toxic Bt genes, or Roundup Ready genes, diversity disappears.

Chemicals kill pollinators and soil organisms. Seventy-five percent of the bees on the planet have disappeared. According to scientists, bees and pollinators contribute more than 159 billion euro annually to agriculture. Chemically farmed soils, sprayed with herbicides and pesticides, kill the beneficial organisms that create soil fertility and protect plants. More than fifty years ago, Rachel Carson wrote *Silent Spring* to wake us up to the ecological destruction caused by pesticides. Organic seeds and organic farming do not just protect human health. They protect the Health and Well-being of all.

With industrial seeds and industrial agriculture, the diversity of plants and crops disappears. Humanity has had 8,500 species of foodstuffs available to consume, and each species has evolved, creating further diversity. India had 200,000 rice varieties before the Green Revolution. This diversity has been replaced by monocultures. Today India grows eight globally-traded commodities. The fastest expanse in acreage is for genetically engineered corn and soya, because they are patented and corporations can collect royalties from farmers. When seed freedom disappears and farmers become dependent on GMO seeds, they in effect become seed slaves. More than 284,000 Indian farmers have committed suicide since seed monopolies were established in India in 1995. Gandhi spun cotton for our freedom. Today GMO Bt cotton has enslaved our farmers in debt and pushed them to suicide. Ninety-five percent of cotton seed is now controlled by Monsanto.

Biodiversity and cultural diversity go hand-in-hand. When culture is eroded, biodiversity is eroded. When control over seed becomes big business, diversity disappears ever faster.

When ecological inputs are replaced with external inputs, diversity becomes a problem, and monocultures become an imperative, since chemically fertilized crops start competing with one another, and because these crops require different external inputs.

Diversity is a product of care, connection, and cultural pride. The mango breeders wanted to give us the best taste, the best quality. So they evolved the diversity of the delicious *dasheri, langra, alphonso* . . .

The tribals and peasants who gave us rice diversity wanted to develop a rice for lactating mothers, a rice for babies, a rice for old people. They wanted to have rices that survive droughts and floods and cyclones, so they evolved climate-resilient rices. In the Himalaya, different rices are needed for different altitudes and different slopes. The intimacy and care that go with belonging to a place and a community allows diversity to flourish. Conserving and growing diversity comes as naturally as breathing.

Greed cannot deal with care; it promotes carelessness. Greed drives control, and control is facilitated through uniformity and monocultures. You cannot control diversity, you can only co-evolve and co-create with it.

A will to control becomes a will to destroy diversity, through what I have called the Monoculture of the Mind. And the expansion of corporate control over seed and plants is the main reason for the disappearance of diversity in our fields and in our food.

Corporations first controlled agriculture through the chemical inputs for the Green Revolution. External chemical inputs demand uniformity and lead to monocultures. In an ecological system wheat and mustard and *chana* (chickpeas) grow in a mixture. An internal input, self-organizing system is based on diversity and cooperation. When ecological inputs are replaced with external inputs, diversity becomes a problem, and monocultures become an imperative, since chemically-fertilized crops start competing with one another, and because these crops require different external inputs. This is how the Green Revolution destroyed the rich diversity of our rice and wheat. It also displaced our *dalhans* (dals) and *tilhans* (oilseeds), without which our agriculture and diets are incomplete. Millets, which we at Navdanya call Forgotten Foods, were driven out of our farms and off our plates on the totally unscientific criteria of being called inferior grains, even though in health and nutrition terms indigenous rice and wheat varieties are superior in nutrition to the new varieties. Native rices have a low glycemic index, while industrial rice has a high glycemic index. When all that the poor get is this industrial rice, they also get diabetes. India has become the capital of diabetes, a disease that is intimately linked to the disappearance of diversity. Native wheats have high protein and do not contribute to gluten allergies. That is why we had to fight the Biopiracy of an ancient wheat by Monsanto, which wanted to monopolize the market for gluten-free wheat products.

Not only does living, organic seed have more quality, nutrition, and taste, farming systems that are based on biodiversity produce more nutrition and "Health per Acre," as the Navdanya study has shown (published by Navdanya / Research Foundation for Science, Technology, and Ecology, 2012, New Delhi). Seed Freedom is the answer to hunger and malnutrition. One billion people today are hungry and two billion are obese because of an agriculture that is out of balance with nature and nature's ecological processes. Half of humanity is thus denied well-being through food.

With globalization, a more expanded and aggressive assault on the diversity of our crops and foods is taking place. There are three forces driving the disappearance of diversity, and all three are connected to corporate control over seed and food.

The first is the entry of big business into the seed market, and the consequent replacement of local varieties developed by farmers with uniform commercial, industrial hybrids and GMOs, sold by corporations. For example, local farmers traditionally grew different watermelon varieties, and watermelons were seasonal fruits. Today you get only one variety everywhere, all year round, produced from seeds that are commercial hybrids. The same applies to papaya.

The second is globalization-driven long-distance trade. Diversity goes hand-in-hand with local, decentralized food systems. Our mangoes and bananas are as diverse as they are because they are eaten fresh, locally.

Long-distance trade replaces freshness and softness with hardness, so that fruits can travel. I call this breeding rocks, not fruit. Our soft-jacket oranges have disappeared and been replaced with varieties that cannot be peeled. Corporations are advising our government that our bananas and mangoes need to travel longer, and stay longer on shelves. I shudder to think of the *dasheri* giving way to the hard, tasteless, flavorless "mango" found in global markets, or the little Kerala banana with the daintiest of skins being driven out by the characterless, thick-skinned Cavendish.

The third is industrial processing. When McDonald's wants potatoes for french fries, only the Russett Burbank will do. Pepsi's Lay's potato chips cannot use indigenous potato varieties like the *tomri* that we grow in the mountains. Ketchup requires tomatoes with pulp, not juice. So the juicy, tasty tomatoes disappear, and hard and tasteless tomatoes replace them. Fortunately, the Italians have continued to grow good and diverse tomatoes since they have pride in their food culture, and have managed to get the Mediterranean diet on the UNESCO heritage list. Similarly, every cuisine in every part of India deserves to be recognized as a cultural heritage. And it is this cultural heritage which supports the biodiversity heritage.

For protecting our biodiversity and food heritage, Navdanya has been making its contributions. But the issue is too important not to be taken up by every citizen in their daily lives. It is too important not to be taken up by spiritual movements. Food begins as seed. The seed is sacred. Food is sacred.

"Annam Brahman"—food is the Creator. We are what we eat. When we are careless with food we are careless with ourselves. Will we wake up only when the last peasant and the last seed disappears? Or will we turn to the sacred duty of protecting our sacred seeds?

SACRED SEED–THE ORTHODOX CHRISTIAN TRADITION

His All Holiness, Bartholomew,
Archbishop of Constantinople,
New Rome and Ecumenical Patriarch

Every seed contains the potential to save the world. Each seed can keep millions of people from starvation. Each seed is a mirror and guardian of the world's future. Each seed is the ecology that can sustain the economy. This is why seeds are sacred and why they are traditionally believed to be miraculous in indigenous circles.

In Christian scripture, theology, and tradition, seeds assume a divine dimension, ascribed to and describing the very Son and Word of God. The divine Word is mysteriously planted in people's hearts, where it calls for proper care and nurture in order to bear fruit. Thus, in the Gospel according to Luke, Jesus Christ tells the following parable:

> A sower went out to sow his seed; and as he sowed, some fell on the path and was trampled on, and the birds of the air ate it up. Some fell on the rock; and as it grew up, it withered for lack of moisture. Some fell among thorns, and the thorns grew with it and choked it. Some fell into good soil, and when it grew, it produced a hundredfold. . . . The seed is the word of God. . . . As for that in the good soil, these are the ones who, when they hear the word, hold it fast in an honest and good heart, and bear fruit with patient endurance. (Luke 8:5–15)

In the early second century of the Christian era, Justin Martyr articulated a theory of the divine Word (or *Logos*) as a seed that germinates the entire world. Therefore, he developed a philosophy demonstrating the permeation of divine seeds as forces that penetrate and saturate the entire world. Justin was convinced that divine truth, beauty, and virtue could be discerned and discovered in every person everywhere.

Seeds are crucial for the life system of our planet. They are beneficial for the healing of disease. They provide fresh oxygen for people to breathe. They radically reduce the human impact on climate change. By growing food organically and at home, we are decreasing our footprint on the planet even more than CO_2 emissions from coal-fired power stations: we eliminate food miles, packaging prices, transportation fuel, and travel costs.

Seeds are crucial for the life system of our planet.

Unfortunately, most people are only used to hearing about global warming, ice caps melting, and CO_2 emissions. Yet, genetically modified foods through the introduction of chemicals into our food supply can equally jeopardize the Earth and our own lives.

It is critical that we listen to the Word of God. It is essential that we listen to the voice of the Earth. It is paramount that we dig deep and plant seeds.

THE SEED OF COMPASSION

His Holiness the 17th Gyalwang Karmapa, Ogyen Trinley Dorje

What is a seed? A seed is something that has the potential of growth inside of it. It offers limitless possibilities for life. In Buddhism, we often talk about the seed of Bodhicitta (*byang chub kyi sems*), the potential for an awakened mind that resides in all sentient beings. This seed is the basis of Buddhist practice— the generation of wisdom and compassion towards all sentient beings. Without Bodhicitta, there can be no enlightenment. And, all of us—no matter who we are and what we have done—hold this seed of Bodhicitta within ourselves.

It seems to me that the Earth is the very embodiment of Bodhicitta—she unconditionally provides the grounds for life and no matter who we are or what we have done, we equally receive compassion from her. It is quite amazing when one thinks about it—that there is oxygen which we can breathe, that there is water which we can drink, and that there is soil on which plants can grow to feed us. Aren't these miracles that we should feel some awe towards? Instead, we are very busy trying to claim the Earth's bounty for ourselves and deprive others in the act. We behave in the exact opposite way to her! And, we are very shocked when there are consequences to our collective actions such as natural disasters, climate change, and wars. Because we spend so little time nurturing the

Bodhicitta seed, we even lack the ability to acknowledge that our actions have brought these troubles to the world.

The food that shows up on our plates, meal after meal, is made available through far-reaching chains of interactions—of many people who have struggled under terrible conditions, of animals that are painfully exploited, and land that has been misused and contaminated. When we eat that food, the least we can do is feel some gratitude to all the beings that have taken part in the process so that we can live. It is essential that we awaken the seed of compassion in ourselves and make ethical choices that minimize the suffering of others, whether it is in giving up meat so that animals do not bear the tremendous suffering they do, eating organic food so that the land and water are not poisoned through the use of fertilizers and pesticides, or by giving support to those who try to protect the rights of poor farmers.

It is very important that we emulate the Earth's attitude of generosity towards us. Just as we would do when receiving a precious gift from someone we love, we need to nurture what we have been given. This includes the Earth's many wonders and biodiversity, as well as our relationship with all sentient beings. It also includes our own minds and our own Bodhicitta seed. We should nurture this precious seed of compassion and give it all the light and nourishment it needs to grow. If we are able to do this, we will no longer simply be a burden upon the Earth but a source of relief.

It is very important that we emulate the Earth's attitude of generosity towards us. Just as we would do when receiving a precious gift from someone we love, we need to nurture what we have been given.

SEEDS OF A NEW HUMANITY

Sister Joan Chittister, OSB

The mystic Julian of Norwich, holding an acorn in her hand in the fourteenth century said of it, "In this is all that is." The Earth shakes at the thought of the simple truth of it.

In every seed lie the components of all life the world has known from all time to now.

In every seed is the reckless, electric, confounding power of creation made new again.

In every seed is the gift of life to those seeking life, wanting life, denied the kind of life that is full of energy, full of hope.

But the hope is a tenuous one, a sacred one, one to be treated with awe for fear of our own failures to protect it.

Seeds are the one thing that are the only genuine promise we have of the future. "Even if I knew that the world would end tomorrow," Martin Luther wrote, "I would plant an apple tree today." It is an insight that defies despair, that promises new life in the midst of the old. It is a beacon that cries out for commitment in an age such as ours when the seeds of destruction among us—greed, power, and control—are in mortal struggle with the seeds of life.

In our time, death is king. The forests die for the sake of loggers. Great fish die for the sake of caviar. The fields die for the sake of fracking. The air dies for the sake of oil. Humanity dies for the sake of money. And people die for want of the food that all these things threaten.

And now, so accustomed have we become to destruction in the name of progress, we are on the brink of commercializing seed, of politicizing seed, of monopolizing seed, of genetically modifying seeds for the sake of someone's control of creation, of making seed the new military weapon of the twenty-first century.

In every seed lie the components of all life the world has known from all time to now.

It is all a matter of valuing the money we can make today more than we value the life that is meant to come.

But the problem is that we ourselves are all seeds, too. We are either seeds of universal love or seeds of exploitative racism. We are seeds of eternal hope or we are seeds of starving despair. We are seeds of a new humanity or we are the harbingers of humanity's decay.

It is a choice. A conscious choice that depends on what we see in seeds and how we treat them and whose we think they are and what we will do to keep them free and available. Or not.

We are the seed of our own life to come and the life of the planet as well. Indeed, "In the seed is everything that is."

SEEDS AND THE STORY OF THE SOUL

Llewellyn Vaughan-Lee

Seeds are what is most essential to life, to our sustenance. For many centuries the planting of the seed in the earth symbolized the mystery of life and the journey of the soul—through a descent into the underworld,* life was regenerated. Through the darkness we are reborn into the light. In our current supermarket life of pre-packaged products, far removed from the cycles of planting, we may have forgotten this mystery; and yet it remains within our psyche as one of the most symbolic and nourishing stories of the soul, a connection with the deeper meaning of our existence. And now as the integrity of the seed is threatened, so is this story and its primal meaning.

The way we live, individually and collectively, tells the story of our soul. The fact that we have to fight for something so essential to life as the integrity of seeds, speaks to the real drama of this present time: that we have to fight to preserve what is most fundamental and sacred to life. We have to protect the Earth and our own soul from a culture that has polluted and desecrated the inner and outer worlds, and that seeks to control life for its own profit and power.

It is vital that we keep the original purity of seeds—that our farms and seed banks preserve this primal source of life. It is also vital that we hold

The fact that we have to fight for something so essential to life as the integrity of seeds, speaks to the real drama of this present time: that we have to fight to preserve what is most fundamental and sacred to life.

in our soul the story of the seed—its symbolic meaning that nourishes our inner self as much as the fruits of the seed nourish our body. Life itself is asking us to save what is most sacred from a civilization that has lost its way, that has lost its connection to the Earth and the symbolic dimension of human beings. We need to remember that the seed and the soul are sacred: they belong to the future as well as to the past. For our children and our children's children we cannot afford to lose this connection, the integrity of this way of being.

But the story of the seed can also give us hope in this darkening time. As we live in the wasteland of a materialistic culture, where amidst its images of abundance we have to search hard for fragments of meaning, the story of the seed tells of a regeneration in the darkness. If we can stay true to the sacred substance and sacred meaning of the seed, it will help us to be a place of rebirth: a place where the inner and outer worlds meet, where real nourishment can once again be born and flower. Working together with the Earth, with its wonder and mystery, we can help in its healing and regeneration.

SEED AS THE COSMIC PRINCIPLE

Swami Veda Bharati

The words for 'seed' are an intrinsic part of human culture. Here we take the Sanskrit word *bija* or *vija* (pronounced beeja or veeja).

It is a word with multiple etymologies and the lexicographers derive it from different verb roots. The meanings derived from these are:

That which takes birth as an offspring.
That which takes birth as the effect of a cause.
That which moves into and in the womb.
Wherewith one frees oneself of debt.
That which is impelled to be effective.

To pull together the ideas presented in these five etymologies:

It is the very seed that becomes its own offspring in a chain of causes and effects. It represents the entire universal principle of causation by becoming enwombed and then presenting itself in a new form. There is a subtle, intangible force within it, a *shakti*, energy-field, that impels it to manifest as an effect. By understanding and applying these principles of the seed one may free oneself of one's karmic debts (for example, a parent is freed of his debt to the ancestors by giving birth to and serving one's offspring as one was served by one's own parents).

Thus the seed principle in the universe encompasses all cosmic processes as well as their applications in one's conduct of life.

Each moment of time carries the potentiality of a seed that unfolds into future events.

In the Bhagavad-gita, the Lord says:

> Know Me to be the perennial seed of
> all beings. (7.10)

In the story of creation as narrated in the Laws of Manu, we read:

> He first created the waters into which he then released
> the Seed (1.8)

On this, the classical commentator Kulluka interprets 'seed' to be the *shakti*, potentiality, creative and generative power.

In Brahma-vaivarta-purana (Ch. 22), Lord Krishna is said to be the *bija*, the seed of all Divine Incarnations (*avataras*).

The traditional Indian word for algebra is *bija-ganita*, the calculations through seeds, where the algebraic symbols are seen as seeds of a geometric or numerical pattern, rather than *anka-ganita*, through numbers. Bhaskaracharya, the mathematician, inventor, and astronomer (twelfth century AD) begins his work on algebra with laudatory verses:

> To That Lord, Mathematics (*ganita*), I prostrate Whom
> the philosophers of Sankhya state to be
> the producer of the Faculty of intelligence (*buddhi*),
> governed by the Existent (*sat*) Consciousness Principle (*purusha*),
> the one unmanifest seed of all that is manifest.
> (Bhaskara's Text, Bija-ganita, Verse 1)

Thus the manifest form of seed conceals the unmanifest potentialities waiting to be realized.

It is further illustrated in the parable of the fruit of *nyagrodha* (*ficus benghalensis*), the tree whose branches grow downwards and take root, an example of the largest tree possible. In Chandogya Upanishad (6.12.1–3) we read this dialogue (paraphrased here):

Father (Uddalaka by name) said: "Bring a *nyagrodha* fruit hither."
Son, Shvetaketu, brought the fruit.
"Break it"—said the father.
"I have broken it"—said the son.
"What do you see inside?"— asked the father.
"Oh, these tiny little seedlings"—replied Shvetaketu.
"Break one of these as well"—commanded the father.
"I have broken one through"—said the son.
"What do you see inside the seed?"—asked the father.
"There is nothing else inside, O blessed one"—replied the son.

To him the father said: "Beloved one, this subtle (power) that you do not see, it is through that (invisible) subtle power in the seed that this great huge *nyagrodha* tree stands. Have faith, beloved one."

"It is this subtle force; all this (universe) consists of this. This is the reality. That is *atman,* the self. That thou art."

(For further elucidation of this metaphor, the reader is advised to refer to the commentary by Shankaracharya for which there is no space here.)

This is the entire Vedic cosmology and metaphysics, all contained in the seed.

This usage of the word is poignant with meaning as certain mono-syllabic mantras of high potency are also called *bija-mantras*. These cannot be translated but represent certain deific powers.

The concept of seed may be used in many metaphors, for example in Shakespeare's *Macbeth* (Act 1, Scene 3) where Banquo says to Macbeth:

> If you can look into the seeds of time
> And say which grain will grow and which will not,
> Speak, then, to me.

If we look at this passage keeping in view all the points we have made above about the concept of 'seed,' it is a profound statement: each moment of time carries the potentiality of a seed that unfolds into future events. Few fortunate ones are endowed with the foresight and insight into this seed-potential of time. No wonder the seeds grow in season only.

Neglect the seed, and we neglect the entire universe, its chains of causes and effects, and the subtle forces that manifest in our very self, for *atman*, the self, in the seed is that through whose power the vast *Vata* tree grows (in Bhagavad-gita 15.1 and Katha Upanishad 6.1).

Understand the seed, and the meaning of the universe, its causes and effects and all processes of manifestation, as well as our ethical duties in life, are revealed to us.

SEEDS OF PROMISE

Rabbi Rami Shapiro

When the God Yah made earth and sky, no plants or herbs appeared in the fields for no rain had yet fallen, and there was no earthling to till the earth. Then dew arose moistening the ground, and the God Yah formed an earthling from the earth and breathed into its nostrils, and the earthling became aware. Genesis 2:4–7

Human beings are the earth becoming self-aware. We are midwives of the garden: tilling the soil that it might breathe and moisten, and through the planting of seed, give birth to new life. Each generation of flora contains the seeds of promise for the next, and it is our task to preserve that promise by protecting those seeds.

In the third century BCE the author of Ecclesiastes urges us to sow seed each morning, even though we cannot be certain it will take root or yield good fruits (Ecclesiastes 11:6). Centuries later Rabbi Jesus taught a similar lesson in the *Parable of the Sower*, who sowed seed even where it could not grow, trusting that some would fall on good soil and take root (Mark 4:3–9). We sow in unknowing, taking nothing for granted; trusting the future without controlling the future.

This emphasis on trust and sowing seed in abundance may be why among all the fruits mentioned in Torah it is the pomegranate with its many seeds that came to be a major Jewish symbol. The pomegranate represented the fertility of the Promised Land. It was the pomegranate that was embroidered on the High Priest's robes (Exodus 28:33–34), and carved into the pillars that stood before Solomon's Temple (I Kings 7:18). Silver representations of the pomegranate adorn the scrolls of Torah.

According to our rabbis the pomegranate has 613 seeds and thus came to represent the yoga of Judaism: the 613 *mitzvot* (practices), each with the potential to awaken one to *d'vekut*, union with God. Our kabbalists, too, looked to the pomegranate as their metaphor for mystical union, a state they called *Pardes Rimonim*, the Garden of Pomegranates, where the infinite seeds of compassion, love, justice, and hope take root in the lives of those who enter it.

Today these seed-based metaphors are less known, and the metaphors that have come to replace them reflect an otherworldly reality independent of seeds, allowing us to entrust earth and sky, seed and harvest to biotech corporations whose "personhood" is soulless, who do not speak for the earth or midwife her abundance, and whose seeds are scarred with ® and $ rather than the ! that reflects the wonder of life.

If we do not reclaim our nature as earth-made-conscious and our purpose as midwives to the garden, the end will be as the beginning: fields will once again lay barren, life-giving rains will not fall, and there will be no earthlings to till the earth or grieve over life's passing.

THE SEED OF LOVE

Pir Zia Inayat-Khan

Indeed it is God who splits open the seed . . .
Qur'an 6:95

Love is like a seed that contains within it the tree called being.
—Sayyid Muhammad Husayni Gisudaraz

In Arabic *hubb* means love and *habb* means seed. These two words are evidently related, as a number of traditional commentators have observed. From this association it becomes apparent, if it was not already so, that love is a kind of seed, and that seeds are natural symbols of love.

In what sense is love a seed? Love is the cause of the whole universe. The Creator said, "I was a hidden treasure and I loved (*ahbabtu*) to be known, so I created the world that I might be known." Like a seed beneath the ground, the Divine Life was at first hidden and unknown. But since Life was also Love, it was disposed to give forth what it contained. As the primal seed germinated and unfurled, the treasure hidden in its hull was revealed in stem, branch, leaf, flower, and fruit—which is to say, in all that appears before our eyes.

In what sense are seeds symbols of love? As seeds come from scented blossoms and sweet fruit, love is the yield of a heart that has ripened. In winter a seed waits quietly, just as love that is true proves its patience.

A seed is small but rich with possibility, like love, which is as humble as it is powerful. Grain nourishes the human body, and love is the food of the human spirit.

Why do these correspondences matter? For millennia, farmers have sown their crops in diverse mosaics, fertilizing them with the manure of cattle.

 In the last century, as we know, this has changed. Today, cattle are confined in factory farms, while in the fields single crops are grown on a monstrous scale by means of a continuous flow of chemical fertilizers, herbicides, and pesticides. The cost of this method to the health of the environment, human beings, and society has been, and continues to be, enormous. To make nature still more subservient to the demands of business, corporations are now extending their dominion to the very interior of seeds.

This is a grave and troubling matter. It calls into question our most fundamental values. Has it come to pass that we no longer hold as sacred the Love that has brought us, and everything, into being? Have we forgotten the holiness of the seed? So it does seem. But I am convinced that when all is said and done, Love will have the last word.

A seed is small but rich with possibility, like love, which is as humble as it is powerful.

A LITTLE SEED OF AWAKENING

Acharya Judy Lief

According to the Mahayana Buddhist tradition, the most fundamental Heritage Seed is the Seed of Awakening, called "Buddha Nature." This seed is said to be the innermost nature of all beings. Like a physical seed, each of us has within us this seed or potential to awaken our inherent wisdom and compassion. When you look at an acorn, it is hard to imagine how such a modest little thing could have within it the potential to be a magnificent oak tree. Likewise, it is hard to trust our own little seed of awakening and its limitless potential. But like an organic seed, the seed of Buddha Nature wants nothing other than to grow and flourish.

Each of us has within us this seed or potential to awaken our inherent wisdom and compassion.

Ordinary seeds need the right combination of soil, water, and climate to grow. Once those conditions are in alignment, the seed will naturally begin to develop. The seed of Buddha Nature is the same. It will lie dormant until the right conditions come together. But once we discover this potential within us, we can water our seed with loving kindness and prepare its bed with mindfulness. When we do so, the growth of the seed of awakening will be effortless and natural.

It is our responsibility to protect both our external seeds and our internal seed of awakening for the benefit of all beings and that of future generations. Our own flourishing and the flourishing of the environment and our fellow beings are inseparably linked. Let us celebrate our good fortune.

SEED OF WISDOM

Swami Atmarupananda

My grandmother's garden was magic for a child: the velvety texture and brilliant color of a pansy, the wonder of a forget-me-not, the delightful herby flavor of crinkly parsley, all coming from seeds, planted in the earth. Dirt itself was alive in her garden: it had texture, smell, earthworms, moisture, and the power to awaken seeds. On a drive through the countryside, my mother would exclaim, "Oh, look at that beautiful dirt!" Such simple influences created a sense of wonder, a sense of respect.

Under these influences, I began to grow things early. My mother gave me seeds and a small plot of ground to prepare. I planted the seeds and—with a child's sense of time—came more than once every day to see if anything was coming up. Among the seeds I planted every year were radish seeds. I didn't then like radishes—too strong for a child's palate—but I loved growing them because they were the quickest to sprout. The wonder of seeing a row of sprouts rising from the soil where I had sown tiny seeds!

A sense of wonder and of respect comes easily to a child: they are the natural state of the child's mind, if not disturbed.

Einstein famously said that science begins with a sense of wonder. The scientist George Washington Carver's attitude was reverence; reverence is simply respect rising from religious wonder.

But the effect of science has too often been the deadening of wonder and reverence, to its own detriment. Yes, the world can be seen as a machine —dull, dead, insentient—and the scientist as a mechanic, manipulating parts. And the world can be seen as two-dimensional information. But a higher view—higher because truer, more inclusive of all levels of understanding—is to see the world as organism. Machines are man-made extensions of the human sensory and motor organs, a model ill-fitted to the actual world. Organisms have internal integrity, identity, a unity above the individual parts.

The mechanical world can be seen as information. The organismic world is one of wisdom.

In that light, what is a seed? Not a dead machine to be manipulated, not just two-dimensional information to be owned and copyrighted, not simply a product to be patented and commercialized. A seed is the transition between life and life, the bridge over death, the denial of non-existence. A seed is the involution of organism. It's the collected wisdom of hundreds of millions of years of evolution; cultivated seed is that plus the collective wisdom of thousands of years of human experimentation.

In the Hindu tradition, the universe itself is reflected in the seed. At long intervals, the universe enters a seed-state, a profound state of involution, of simplicity, out of which once again the infinitely diverse universe springs forth. But there is the ultimate Seed beyond even that: Truth, *satyam*; pure, luminous Being. That is the Seed of all, and the foundation of wonder.

A HAUDENOSAUNEE REFLECTION ON "SEED: THE POWER OF LIFE"

Dr. Dan Longboat
Roronhiakewen (He Clears the Sky)
Turtle Clan, Mohawk Nation of the Haudenosaunee Confederacy at the Grand River Territory

We are Haudenosaunee "The People of the Longhouse" or *"they who build the house."* This is more than a metaphor for the Six Nations of Indigenous Peoples brought together by the Great Laws of Peace. Building the Longhouse is about actively maintaining our sacred relationship with all of Creation. Our Elders tell us that the Longhouse roof is the Sky World, the eastern and western doors are the rising and setting Sun and the floor is the Mother Earth. We are the Indigenous People of the Eastern Great Lakes of Turtle Island, also known as North America. We are "Corn, Beans and Squash" People. They are Tyonnhehkwen *"we depend on them"* and they are our sustainers. We call these the Three Sisters. Our ancient relationship to Seeds is at the very center of our culture from Planting to Harvest Ceremonies. All of our Longhouse Ceremonies involve giving thanks for the unfolding of Creation and for Seeds, which are the essence of the Natural Law that ensures all Life will continue.

Our oral tradition tells us about the origins of Life beginning in the Sky World and the creation of the Earth. We hear about the relationships between the Sky World Beings and of how a pregnant Sky Woman fell through a hole in the Sky. As she fell, she held in her hands roots, seeds and plants from the Sky World. With the help of the Water Beings who placed mud on a great Turtle's back, Sky Woman danced Turtle Island into being. Then she gave birth to a daughter, the first Being born on the Earth. This daughter grew quickly and soon gave birth to twin boys. One twin had a good mind and worked to create and sustain Life. The other had a different mind focused on destruction and death. Both of them are necessary to maintain balance for the continuation of Life. After Sky Woman's daughter passed away during childbirth, her body was placed inside the Earth along with the Seeds from the Sky World. She became Our Mother the Earth. From Her grave blossomed our sacred Tobacco, Corn, Beans and Squash, Strawberries and Potatoes. Like those from our own physical mothers, these gifts from Our Mother give us life. They nurture and sustain us, physically and spiritually.

For us, Life begins with Woman, and the power of the sacred feminine along with her Seeds are at the centre of all Life. In recognizing, honoring and celebrating this, we *"who build the house"* focus on creating and sustaining Life. We are bound in a sacred reciprocal relationship with Seeds. We depend on them and they depend on us. Their life is our life. We have been tied together for thousands of generations. In our Ceremonies, we thank them and ask that they continue to fulfill their ancient responsibility to sustain us and come to fruition once again. Seeds are Life and sustaining Life is what it means to be Haudenosaunee.

THE SACRED BOND

Sobonfu Somé

At the core of the world is the power of the sacred. It holds all things together in life, and gives each species a sense of identity and purpose. Without the sacred there is no meaning to life. All our relationships reside within this sacred bond. It is the root of our well-being and that which seeds the soul. In sum, it is a divine blessing, a miracle of life that gives us the capacity to procreate. Throughout our existence this sacred alliance will be our compass. Thus, every day we dance to the tune of this sacred song that is never ending, to bring balance and meaning to life.

Because of the nature of our constitution, we have been gifted with a diversity of seeds and nutrients to ensure our survival. These gifts are not about reinforcing our human propensity to dominate; rather they are about how we can learn to be a steward, within the sacred contract. It is only when we can humble ourselves enough to bow to this sacred contract that our survival is assured.

Traditionally, indigenous people have known that the seeds gifted to them are the direct translation of the love and trust of the divinities. Thus, they have never considered these gifts possessions or something to be taken for granted. They know that they are dependent on the welfare of this sacred bond, and work to keep it viable. Because they also know that neglectful actions, beliefs, and behaviors can break or disrespect the sacred bond, which is an invitation for ill to set in, so before planting their fields, rites are performed to invoke the divine alliance and to seek their blessings. Throughout the growing season continuous prayers are sent out to maintain the sacred bond between the natural world and humankind. The same thing is done at harvest. Before the new crops are consumed samples of each crop from the various fields are taken to the village shrine to be offered to the divinities with gratitude, so that they may bless the fruit of the collective labor and ensure prosperity. A feast of gratitude is also offered inviting the divinities to do their sacred dance as the villagers celebrate with them. These rites take place every year to remind us that we are but part of a larger world whose gifts must be respected.

At the core of the world is the power of the sacred.

THE SACRED MYSTERY OF PHYSIS:
HONORING SEED IN ANCIENT GREECE

Christoph Quarch, PhD

The cradle of western civilization once stood in the ancient sanctuary of Delphi. There, at the bottom of Mount Parnassus, in the antique temple of Apollo, a female priest called Pythia gave the god's oracles to those who were in need of guidance. She sat on a tripod, surrounded by sacred smoke emanating from a crack in the Earth. These vapors were considered to be the inspiring breath of the Great Goddess herself—the goddess called Gaia, the Eldest, the Mother of all Gods.

This image is significant, for in the ancient Greek's understanding life was a kind of breeze deriving from below. It was the sacred breath called *yuch* (psyche)—a word we usually translate as "soul"—that animated and gave life to every creature. And it was considered to be a gift of the Earth, of Gaia, the Mother. The mysterious way the Goddess processed the constant generation and withdrawal of life was called *fusis* (physis)—a word we usually (wrongly) translate as "nature."

The physical manifestation of the nous spermaticos—*as it was called by later mystics—was assumed to be the seed. Therefore the seed was considered to be sacred: a sacred embodiment of the omnipresent cosmic intelligence, which by the nutrition and care of Gaia unfolds and grows into the world of existence.*

For *physis* is much more than nature. *Physis* is the essence of being. *Physis* is the divine unfolding of a plant, which once fertilized in the dark womb of the Earth, starts on its own to grow towards the light, entering the infinite space and nevertheless preserving its genuine identity. This, however, is only one half of the miracle, for whatever enters the sphere of existence follows the sacred laws of Gaia: to strive for balance and harmony, to integrate itself into the all-embracing melody of life.

To the Greek mindset it was obvious that the constant come-and-go of appearance and disappearance was directed by the divine intelligence of life itself—an intelligence they called *nous*. According to the teachings of philosophers such as Anaxagoras, Socrates, and Plato, divine *Nous* restlessly arranges and stabilizes the inner harmony of the kosmos: the one and beautiful universe. And they also thought that within everything having come to existence there is a spark of this cosmic intelligence—a kind of individual gravitation spot, a self-organizing principle that preserves the inner structure and arrangement of every single entity.

The physical manifestation of the *nous spermaticos*—as it was called by later mystics—was assumed to be the seed. Therefore the seed was considered to be sacred: a sacred embodiment of the omnipresent cosmic intelligence, which by the nutrition and care of Gaia unfolds and grows into the world of existence.

Heraclitus, a famous philosopher from the sixth century BC, once taught: *physis philei kryptesthai*—"Life loves to hide away." Perhaps by these obscure words he wanted to say that humans usually have little understanding of the miracle of *physis*. Existence is taken for granted while the very cause of existence is ignored. This might be the reason why, in the course of western philosophy, the reverence for life declined. Initiated by Aristotelean metaphysics and inspired by Christian theology, the modern mindset denied the miracle of *physis* and proclaimed production as the only cause of existence. Instead of honoring the very intelligence within eternal nature, thinkers like Descartes declared the human mind to be the only owner of intelligence and by this justified the human claim to be the very *maître et possesseur de la nature*: the master and possessor of nature.

The philosophical transformation by which ancient *physis* turned into modern nature seems to be the basic reason for the fatal abuse of the natural world in our times. However, genetic engineering is the most impudent offspring of a modern mindset full of ignorance and presumption. In the eyes of the original and initial western thinkers in ancient Greece, current biotechnology can only be renounced as a symptom of most self-destructive *hybris*. Therefore it's time for the west to reconnect with its own ancient spiritual roots. And to remember its own birth from the womb of Mother Gaia.

THE SEED–THE SOURCE

Sister Jayanti

The seed is the source of all life. It is something we have to protect and nurture, in order to preserve life for the future.

In every ceremony in India seeds or grains are thrown into sacrificial fires for purification, for worship, or to call forth abundance or auspicious omens. The seed is a symbol of sustenance, nourishment, prosperity, and well-being.

However, there is also a deeper understanding of the seed—that of the Creator of the human world tree. The essence of our spiritual teachings is our connection with God, the Supreme Soul, the Seed—Shiva. The word 'Shiva' means 'the Seed,' 'the Creator,' and also 'the Point' (of light) and 'the Benefactor.'

We understand Shiva to be the eternal and infinite Source of Goodness and Truth, available to all, giving benefit to all, the All-powerful, All-knowing, All-merciful One—the Mother and Father of all humanity.

Just as we experience the soul, the spiritual being, as a point of light situated in the middle of the forehead, just between the eyes, so too, we experience Shiva, God, to be a Point of pure spiritual energy. Raja Yoga ('the sovereign yoga') is that powerful and blissful connection between soul and Supreme Soul, child and Parent.

The essence of our spiritual teachings is our connection with God, the Supreme Soul, the Seed—Shiva. The word 'Shiva' means 'the Seed,' 'the Creator,' and also 'the Point' (of light) and 'the Benefactor.'

When we connect our minds in a loving and natural relationship with God, we are able to fill ourselves with God's power and love and light. God's power and purity give us the strength to transform ourselves: to remove the weakness and negativity within that we have accumulated on our journey and to allow our innate qualities of peace, love, happiness, purity, and wisdom to emerge once again. God reawakens us to our own truth and empowers us to bring these qualities into our lives in a practical way.

In this way, God, Shiva, is the Seed of life, the Source of life and the Energy that transforms old into new, that purifies the whole world and the whole human family, and creates again a world of natural harmony, peace, and beauty.

Through our connection with the Supreme Seed, we begin to see the world as being sacred and our role in the world as one of supporting life and living in harmony with creation. Since all life springs from the seed, it is very important to hold the seed sacred and preserve the original seeds that are still around. To this end the Brahma Kumaris have created a seed bank at their Spiritual Headquarters in Mount Abu, Rajasthan, India.

SEEDS OF THE SPIRIT:
A CALL TO SPIRITUAL ACTION
FOR MOTHER EARTH
A HAUDENOSAUNEE REFLECTION

Kahontakwas Diane Longboat
Turtle Clan, Mohawk Nation from Six Nations
Grand River Territory, Canada

CREATION: SEEDS FILLED WITH LIFE FORCE
FROM THE SPIRIT WORLD FALL TO THE EARTH

Ancient Haudenosaunee oral tradition reveals that Original Creation and the life force within evolution are complementary physical powers. The sacred origins of life and the seeds that came to the Earth from the Spirit World entered this world embedded with the Original Instructions from the Creator for human responsibility to care for all life-forms; the Plan of the Creator for His Creation called Mother Earth; and the balance required in all relationships among Human Beings and all of the life-forms of Creation, none more important than the others. The Divine is present in all of Creation; the origin and principle of life is the ultimate miracle in the majesty and grandeur of natural law.

The sacred role of Woman as Life Giver and Life Bearer is clear. Singing the land to life with song and the gentle patting of feet as Sky Woman did is still practiced in most traditional Indigenous societies as women plant in the spring. The songs sung to the growing plant life were honor songs, welcoming life in the new cycle and thanking the seeds, and the emerging sustenance from those seeds, that will feed our children and families. The new Earth, originally populated by Spirit Beings, here from a holy place, is humbled by the knowledge that we, the living, are their descendants. This fact implies our royal lineage and our immense responsibility to continue to enhance and protect sacred creation in all of its forms.

Diversity is part of the natural law of Mother Earth. Diverse climates, environmental conditions, and geographical locations cause differentiation to thrive. Unity in diversity and the horizontal interdependent order of life-forms is circular not vertical, a lesson well known in the plant world, and is one of the great lessons for humanity. We need to remember that each element of creation, from the plants and animals to the water life and bird life, all have wisdom and medicines to offer to humanity and to each other.

The greatest messages of this era will come from Mother Earth, her creatures, the weather patterns, the light, the shifting of the magnetic fields and axis, and the waters.

The voice of Mother Earth is within the children of this planet.

COUNCIL OF CREATION: THE EGO PLANET

When sectors of humanity denied a connection to the Creator, they became dominated by ego, personal aggrandizement, and greed. Human

Beings became unbalanced, destructive, mind-dominated, and disconnected from the land and severed from a relationship with living beings. With childlike indulgence, they ravaged the planet seeking personal gain at the expense of all the spiritual and natural laws of the Earth.

Today we are witness to the Old Mind struggling to hold on to symbols of the past as measures of security, power, money, and control. It will not be easy to witness the great shift as aggressive behavior and mental illness take hold in those seeking to maintain the status quo. Many will not embrace change in a healthy manner. Those who are fearful will grasp at the symbols and fight to hold them in place. The Old Mind will be removed through love and prayer, not force or violent confrontation.

The western monopoly capitalist paradigm that allows big money to chase after more for the profit of the few, using Mother Earth as a disposable factor of production, is neither sustainable nor logical based on modern science and natural law. Endless economic growth based on finite natural resources is finished. It is a mind-centered egotistical fantasy to thrive at the expense of other Nations. The death of this paradigm has already begun.

The global system of colonialism, racism, and hegemony causing vertical ordering of human cultures and languages has failed. The collapse of whole countries such as the Soviet Union, the global changes in climate that are now determinants of survival, the unending economic recession affecting North America and Europe, now point to the urgency of new

We must remember as Human Beings that we are the seed of the union of love between the Creator and Mother Earth.

forms of knowledge, values, and economies based on natural law, underpinned by spiritual integrity. The vast affairs of the world and the web of resources have been determined by imperialist interests for hundreds of years. Now the time has come for Indigenous paradigms to step forward with synergistic solutions for the highest common good and welfare of all living organisms.

Knowledge to renew the life purpose of humanity is embedded in traditional Indigenous wisdom on the secrets of life, grounded in community, with Keepers of sacred knowledge and environmental edicts that stand on the shoulders of unbroken generations of Ancestors in alignment with the Creator's teachings and the natural laws of Mother Earth. Millions of years of human history and evolution are part of the knowledge base of these new/old scholars whose minds have been trained since birth and whose souls have never been conquered by western imperialism.

Today those responsible for environmental degradation face environmental karma, not only for themselves but for their children and the generations of their family yet unborn if they do not realign with natural law and spiritual law.

The process of genetic alteration of seeds or the DNA of animals is squarely contradictory to natural law and evolution. The natural law of Mother Earth will not be degraded in perpetuity. The great lessons that humanity must learn will be learned on this planet. As our Hopi relatives warn, this is the fourth world and the last opportunity for humanity to

42

come to terms with compassion, love, balance, reciprocity, gratitude, humility, and truth, and apply them to the workings of daily living.

ERA OF LIVING SPIRIT: SEED OF THE NEW MIND

Today we find ourselves in the era of Living Spirit foretold in prophecy among many Nations of Indigenous peoples worldwide. Prophecy is remembering, and placing the seeds of remembrance before the people to engage a process of deep memory embedded in our DNA of the Original Instructions given to the human families on how to be in a loving, just, and reciprocal relationship with all elements of creation.

We have lost our way, we must return to the beginning.

We must remember as Human Beings that we are the seed of the union of love between the Creator and Mother Earth. The oldest lifeways on the planet are Indigenous, and are found throughout the Earth from southeast Asia, Japan, the Polynesian Islands, Aotearoa, the Americas, the continent of Africa, Europe, India, the cold reaches of Scandinavia and Russia to the plains of Mongolia. Within these Indigenous paradigms are the secrets of life, held at the Sacred Fires, the Seat of the Spirit.

A universal language of the land and the Spirit World is common to all who live in balance with Natural Law and Spiritual Law, universal and unifying. The messages of the Ancestors in dreams and visions have guided the pathway. It has been a long journey for all of creation to reach this era. Many spiritual messages and events have lead us as a human family to this moment, when the birth of the White Buffalo in North

America opened the door to the hope for humanity, and the presence of the Great Winds opened the human mind to the prophecies unfolding, foretelling the future.

This is the time to focus on the children and the unborn with a view to the world they will inherit. The children carry the seeds of the Spirit for the unfolding of the New Mind. The spiritual evolution of the human being has been foretold in the prophecies of the Ancestors.

Plant seeds contain the story of creation, the spiritual law for the continuance of life, the natural law for relationship with the sun, winds, air, water, rains, microorganisms, minerals of the soil, and other companion plants. To alter them is to disobey the laws of the Creator. Their integrity is the inherited legacy for the generations of the unborn. It is our duty to return the seeds to the coming generations in the same state as the seeds were gifted to us.

YOUR ACTION PLAN:
* Plant our family or community gardens with ancient grains and heritage seeds.
* Make shopping lists of products we do not buy because they contain GMO ingredients.
* Become Activists to educate the public and pressure our governments to label the food products having GMO ingredients.
* Encourage land-based learning for children as essential to connect them to the land and for the spirits of the Ancestors on the land to inspire them as they learn.
* Self-educate to understand how GMOs contribute to human disease.

- Provide courses on nutrition with whole organic foods as disease-fighting mechanisms; food is your medicine.
- Witness soils depleted of minerals and microorganisms for years after chemicals have burned the life force out of them during the GMO farming process; witness crop failure when GMO crops experience floods, droughts, or other adverse weather conditions, molds, infestations.
- Learn to cook whole foods, organic, local, and in season; avoid processed, frozen, canned, microwave foods, meats from factory farms.
- Understand that food sovereignty is your right; no Nation can be self-determining if they are dependent on outside sources to feed their people.
- Return to a relationship with the land where, as humans, we fall in love with all of creation, and we protect what we love.

SEEDS AND THE SACRED

Mary Ann Burris

In Native American spirituality, in Nature and in culture, seeds are the future and they are the past. They are ancestors and offspring. They are the circle of life. The Three Sisters of corn, squash, and beans were a gift from the Divine Creator, to be cherished and nurtured generation to generation. When we nurture them, they nurture us. It is a circle.

> *Humankind has not woven the web of life.*
> *We are but one thread within it.*
> *Whatever we do to the web, we do to ourselves.*
> *All things are bound together.*
> *All things connect.*
> —Chief Seattle, 1854

In Buddhist teachings, each of us has the same 51 seeds in our soil, in our store of consciousness. These seeds include faith, energy, humility, wisdom, zeal, mindfulness, and peacefulness. They also include greed, craving, pride, sloth, gloom, and selfishness. These seeds are in all of us as potentialities. Our mental formations, our characters, are shaped by the seeds that are nurtured in our lives. We can consciously attend to our healthy seeds, those connected to love. We can water our unhealthy seeds, those connected to fear. Our surroundings influence the seeds that are strong in us, but it is our spirit, our consciousness, that shapes our lives, that helps us know that we are One and to live each day in that knowing.

Our surroundings influence the seeds that are strong in us, but it is our spirit, our consciousness, that shapes our lives, that helps us know that we are One and to live each day in that knowing.

For the past few years at TICAH (Trust for Indigenous Culture and Health), we have produced a "Good Seeds/Mbegu Njema" calendar. Each month, the lead is a "good seed" in our hearts (patience, peace, joy, unity, good judgment, vision). Each month there are also "good seeds" in our Constitution, in our gardens (in the form of an herbal remedy), in our sharing (in the form of questions for discussion), and in our histories and cultures (dates, quotes, art). In very practical ways, in the slums of Nairobi, our seeds are our health.

What I know from Nature, from my practice and my vision, from my own hybrid spiritual tradition—Christian, Native, Jewish, Buddhist—is that seeds are sacred. They are the central metaphor for who we are and how we act in the world, how we cherish what is passed down to us, how we live today, and how we take care of what is to come. Are biotechnology companies watering the seeds of wisdom? Are they watering the seeds of greed? Are we? This, too, is a circle.

Seeds are connection, fertility. To destroy them is not only to damage ourselves, but to diminish the planet's storehouse. It is to harm those who crawl, who fly, who swim, who run, whose roots are still. What is needed instead is to recognize our wild relations, to respect all our relations.

As Hale Makua, Hawaiian elder and teacher, used to say, "We must RE-MEMBER. We must connect, bring together, bring to life. Again and again and again."

THERE IS NO LIFE WITHOUT A SEED AND THERE IS NO SEED WITHOUT A LIFE

Venerable Bhante Buddharakkhita

"Though I do not believe that a plant will spring up where no seed has been, I have great faith in a seed. Convince me that you have a seed there, and I am prepared to expect wonders."
—Henry David Thoreau

A seed is a small embryonic plant enclosed in a covering called the seed coat, usually with some food store. It is a critical state in the life cycle of plants, and increases the chances of plants' dispersion and colonization of new areas. This distribution mechanism reduces competition among the seedlings and guarantees survival of the offspring.

MAJOR IMPORTANCE OF A SEED

In a spiritual context, a seed is seen as the ideological beginning of a thought. In the animal kingdom, the idea of the seed in plants is a perfect analogy of an egg.

The seed encodes the genetic message of the parent plants in a perfect manner that conserves all their

49

characteristics and assures the survival of a particular plant species from one generation to another, even in periodically unfavorable conditions. When a seed lands in the right conditions it grows and bears fruits; when it lands in unfavorable conditions it dries and dies.

The seed has unique inherent survival abilities that can remain dormant for as long as undesirable conditions like drought, winter, and so on persist, which could otherwise cause the extinction of a plant species. When favorable conditions return, the seed triggers growth hormones initiating metabolic activities that cause the rapid multiplication of the plant's cells, setting growth into motion.

The Buddha likened types of seeds to wrong or right views. He said that when a nimb-tree seed is placed in moist soil, whatever nutriment it takes from the soil and the water is conducive to its bitterness and distastefulness. Even so, when someone has wrong views, whatever action, speech, or thought one engages is conducive to bitterness. On the other hand, when a grape seed is placed in moist soil, whatever nutriment it takes from the soil and the water, all is conducive to its sweetness. Even so, when someone has a right view, whatever action, speech, or thought one engages is conducive to sweetness. Therefore, possessing the right view is a very important seed for cultivating the path to final awakening or liberation.

THE PRESERVATION OF A SEED
Knowing the importance of a seed, the Buddha offered ways of preserving them. A cursory examination of the Vinaya Pitaka (the basket of monastic

disciplinary rules) reveals the lengths to which the Buddha went in his mission to cement an ethic of non-violence, compassion, and environmental responsibility. Through dedication to the protection of all living creatures as well as plants and seeds, the monastic rules provide an organic response that frames deep compassion for the natural world as both a spiritual and ecological necessity. The Buddhist monastic code also contains guidelines for the use of plant seeds.

The Vinaya Pitaka states: *"If [the monk] thinks that it is a seed, when it is a seed, (and) cuts it or has it cut or breaks it or has it broken or cooks it or has it cooked, there is an offense of expiation. If he thinks that it is not a seed when it is a seed (and) cuts it (and so on) . . . there is no offense. If he thinks that it is a seed when it is not a seed, there is an offense of wrong-doing. If he thinks that it is not a seed when it is not a seed, there is no offense."* This clearly demonstrates the role of intention, or *cetana*, in determining whether or not an offense is committed. In addition to these rules, the Buddha did not allow his monks or nuns to accept fresh and uncooked grains in order to prevent the destruction of seeds; fruits are allowable only if *"damaged by fire, by a knife, by a finger-nail; [or if] it is seedless or its seed(s) are removed."*

The Dhamma (the truth taught by Buddha) has symbolically been called the seed, as in the book *Planting Dhamma Seeds in Africa* by Venerable Buddharakkhita, meaning that all the attributes of a seed can be likened to the Dhamma as: *Medicine and food to us, the way to pass on good life from generation to generation, the word that harnesses our living environment, the word of wisdom that ushers in happiness, peace, and well-being of the world around us, which if it died, would leave the world in a state of extinction.*

LISTENING TO THE HIDDEN HEART OF SEEDS

Angela Fischer

Every seed carries a secret.

We will never come to fully know this secret, because it belongs to the mystery of creation. Yet we can learn again what hundreds of generations did before us, namely to live with the secrets, to use them as gifts, and to honour them as a source of life on this planet.

The first step in learning to live with a secret is to listen.

When I was a young child, my mother gave me a seed of a bean. She showed me how to plant it into a pot filled with black soil and how to keep it warm and moist. And then I had to wait.

For a young child this took a very long time. Every morning I would visit my seed, invisible in the darkness of the soil, and because I could not see anything, I remember that instead I tried to hear something. It was around the same time that my mother was pregnant, and I used to put my ear to her belly to communicate with the baby I could not see or touch. So I did the same with the invisible seed: I put my ears close to the soil and listened. I do not remember if I ever heard something, but I remember the listening. It was like an intimate conversation, though silent and unheard by anyone else.

The seed is a symbol for the deepest mystery of creation, and at the same time it is the mystery. For thousands of years farmers have known how to listen to these mysteries, and so found ways how to grow and to harvest, how to preserve the seeds, how to provide for them the best circumstances, considering the conditions of the earth, the soil, and the weather, and considering how much they connect us with the past and the future, our ancestors and our grandchildren. This goes back to an ancient feminine wisdom about the connection with the Earth, the knowledge of light being born out of darkness and an intimacy with the circles of life.

Every seed contains a light. Through greed and disconnection from the sacredness of life, this light is threatened. Genetically modified seeds become sterile. If the fertility is removed from a seed, its light is taken away; it withdraws. The divine light that is present in every seed is manifested through its fertility, through the potential to grow and to be a source for new life. When this light withdraws from a seed, it withdraws from the whole of creation, and our souls begin to starve.

As every seed embraces an outer as well as an inner reality, we need to care in outer and in inner ways. We need to protect the purity, diversity, and freedom of seeds through outer engagement, but we also need to protect the sacredness of life inwardly. The inner way is to hold the awareness of the sacredness in our hearts, to remember and to respect the feminine mysteries of creation—and to deeply listen. The same light that is contained in the heart of the biological seed is also present within our heart; it is the seed of love.

AND THE LAST SHALL BE FIRST

Shailly Barnes, Adam Barnes, Rev. Liz Theoharis, and Rev. Kathy Maskell: Poverty Initiative at Union Theological Seminary, NYC

The theology of the Bible does not tolerate any disrespect for God's creation. In the Book of Genesis and throughout the Old and New Testaments, God commissions people to be stewards of creation and protectors of life so that we may thrive, not merely survive. Therefore, any system that attempts to compete with God by controlling the means for sustaining life—seed, food, water, land, and medicine—is, by Biblical standards, idolatrous. In the Christian tradition, this is most dramatically revealed through the life, death, and resurrection of Jesus Christ. Jesus presents a radical and defining counter-narrative to the prevailing exploitative systems of power by declaring that "the last shall be first,"[1] and that all life is sacred.

Thus, we ought not to be impressed with the wealth that the giants of agribusiness have amassed in the presence of poverty today. What we must pay attention to is that this wealth was acquired on the backs of the poor. The extension of intellectual property rights over seeds facilitates a concentration of the resources and wealth required to sustain human life in very few hands and is directly related to the massive debt, displacement, and dispossession of the masses. This reveals the great disregard that this system has for human life: it not only produces poverty, but relies on poverty to grow.

Forty years ago, the Rev. Dr. Martin Luther King, Jr., channeled the same biblical call for justice and critique of the powers that be when he launched the Poor People's Campaign. He declared:

> The dispossessed of this nation . . . must organize a revolution . . . against the structures through which the society is refusing to take means which have been called for, and which are at hand, to lift the load of poverty. . . . There are millions of poor people in this country who have very little, or even nothing, to lose. If they can be helped to take action together, they will do so with a freedom and a power that will be a new and unsettling force in our complacent national life. . . . Those who choose to join . . . this "freedom church" of the poor, will . . . develop nonviolent action skills.[2]

King's campaign continues through the Poverty Initiative's network of Poverty Scholars—leaders and organizations in 26 states in the United States and 17 countries around the world—who are waging daily struggles against this system.[3] Their fights reflect the prophetic "power, justice, and courage" to call out these injustices, knitting together the fabric of a vibrant social movement that affirms the arc of God's justice and laws.[4]

This emerging "new and unsettling force" is a present-day illustration of the parable of the mustard seed, which Jesus used to teach about the unexpected places and ways that the kingdom of heaven is realized on earth.[5] Together, as poor people from every race and place in America and all walks of life, we take up King's challenge to build the new freedom church of the poor in hope and with determination. Membership is open to all.

---

1 Matthew 19:30, "But many who are first will be last; and the last, first."

2 Martin Luther King, Jr., "A Time to Break the Silence," April 4, 1967, reprinted in *A Testament of Hope*.

3 Poverty Scholars organizations working most directly in the area of food and agricultural justice include Brazil's Landless Workers' Movement (Movimento dos Trabalhadores Rurais Sem Terra or MST), who have revisioned what the right to food is and can be by making the explicit connections between land, livelihood, dignity, and freedom; the Coalition of Immokalee Workers (CIW) in Florida—an organization of nearly 4000 agricultural workers—whose struggle against poverty wages and slavery in the tomato fields explicitly raises the contradictions of wage labor in a highly mechanized food system, where men and women must compete with machines to maximize profits for corporations; Poughkeepsie Farm Project, which is working to build a just and sustainable food system to address the widespread poverty and lack of healthful foods in Poughkeepsie, New York; and Restaurant Opportunities Center-NYC, which organizes restaurant workers who confront wage theft and other violations in the workplace. More broadly, in his lifetime, Larry Gibson—the Keeper of the Mountain in West Virginia—fought some of the most aggressive proprietors of natural resources in the global economy as he struggled to protect both his ancestral home of Kayford Mountain from mountaintop removal and his family's rights to health, water, air, and environment; likewise, "Water Warriors" Marion Kramer and Maureen Taylor of the Michigan Welfare Rights Organization are pushing back against the privatization of water in Detroit, Michigan, a process that has contributed to the rising costs of water and utilities, water shut-offs, foreclosures, and broken families.

4 Micah 3:8–9, "But truly I am filled with power—with the Spirit of the Lord—and with justice and courage. . . . Hear this, you leaders . . . who despise justice and distort all that is right."

5 Mark 4:30, "And Jesus said, 'How shall we picture the kingdom of heaven, or by what parables shall we present it? It is like a mustard seed, which, when sown upon the soil, though it is smaller than all the seeds that are upon the soil, yet when it is sown, it grows up and becomes larger than all the garden plants and forms large branches; so that the birds of the air can nest under its shade.'"

SEEDS AND THE MIRACLE OF LIFE

Aliaa Rafea, PhD

In Islam, gratefulness is the main character of believers around which all other ethics revolve. The first chapter in Qur'an starts with praising Allah, the Lord of the Worlds, the Most Merciful and Compassionate. Acknowledging the Mercy of the Divine is a way to show gratefulness to everything that exists, including the gift of life that is bestowed upon humans. In Islam, it is through raising the awareness of natural bounty, balance and beauty, that humans came to realize the divine aspect as manifested within everything, "wherever you go, you encounter the presence of the Divine."

> And He it is Who produces gardens (of vine), trellised and un-trellised, and palms and seed-produce of which the fruits are of various sorts, and olives and pomegranates, like and unlike; eat of its fruit when it bears fruit, and pay the due of it on the day of its reaping, and do not act extravagantly; surely He does not love the extravagant.
> (Holy Qur'an 6:141)

Humans are asked to know about the universe and use their knowledge to keep the balance. They are taught that seeds are the source of life in all creatures. "A Sign for them is the earth that is dead, We do give it a life, We brought about seeds that they can eat" (HQ 36:33).

Qur'an also draws the attention to watch the relationship between different phenomena: "is He Who sends the winds like heralds of glad tidings, going before His mercy: when they have carried the heavy-laden clouds, We drive them to a land that is dead, make rain to descend thereon, and produce every kind of harvest therewith" (HQ 7:57).

Qur'an advises humans to appreciate the miracle of creation. Regardless of how much we are able to know about genes, there will remain aspects about life and death that will remain unknown to us. It is awesome to think of the majesty of how "seeds" go into a magnificent process and complete their journey to maintain the continuity of their own kind. It is equally mysterious to watch the process of aging and dying. It is even more miraculous to become aware of the capabilities that humans enjoy, both to what extent they can improve the natural condition, and how they can destroy life on Earth by their lust, greed, and selfishness. "The likeness of what they spend in the life of this world is as the likeness of wind in which is intense cold (that) smites the seed produce of a people who have done injustice to their souls and destroys it; and Allah is not unjust to them, but they are unjust to themselves" (HQ 3:117).

From this perspective, interfering with the genetic makeup of seeds, animals or humans could have adverse consequences, if not done with care. There must be a backup for all seeds as they originated in the natural world. If we understand that our lives sprang from "seeds" (sperm and eggs united), and cannot continue without seeds, then we will understand that we have to be careful about the seed from which everything was created.

THE DNA OF OUR SOUL CANNOT BE GENETICALLY MODIFIED!

Swami Omkarananda

When we think of human evolution we generally consider physical form, and science has shown that genetics is the main mechanism behind this evolutionary process. Yoga, the great spiritual science of the East, focuses on the evolution of human consciousness as well as form—form cannot evolve without consciousness. *Karma* (meaning action) and rebirth are the means by which this consciousness evolves.

Our physical body (form) has its underlying genetic code (DNA) and the soul also has its specific "karmic code." The soul carries karmic "seeds," called *samskaras*, from one body to the next (reincarnation). These *samskaras* ripen in the soil of our lives, taking root and sprouting according to prevailing conditions. Thus the soul's karmic code is based on the habits, tendencies, influences, and desires set into motion over its many births.

As the great Vedic scholar David Frawley elucidates so elegantly, the unfolding of our own human karma is part of the evolution of consciousness on the planet. As an evolutionary force karma is the self-rectifying power of the self-creating universe. Karmic law teaches us that our individual actions are linked to the fate of the entire world. Ecologically, this should make us responsible for all that we do, both to ourselves and to others. As we act, so the world reacts and shapes us in return. A spiritual or "yogic ecology" has to be based on an understanding of the law of karma and it requires us to recognize our unity with the All and develop a consciousness of the sacred basis for all our interactions.

From a yogic point of view, therefore, nature is not dead matter to shape to our will, but the expression of sacred Self in the physical world. If we forget this ecological basis of spirituality, we will lose our foundation in the Earth that provides the support for our journey back to the light.

Ideally we should understand the unfolding of our karma as an opportunity to experience our interconnectedness with the conscious Universe—we need to live the life of a soul that is one with all life. We urgently need to respond to the evolutionary message of our karma by taking responsibility for our actions and seeing all creatures as our own Self, remembering that the Self in all is eternal and not subject to "genetic modification"!

Thus, a number of yogis are now seeing their discipline connected to that of permaculture, the science of respectful relation in the physical universe. To address the idea of genetically modifying seeds from a yogic or vedantic point of view would take volumes, not one book and certainly not a short essay. All I can do is to suggest a different way of looking at this . . . to plant a seed, so to speak, which hopefully will blossom into an exploration of this huge topic.

THE POWER AND IMPORTANCE OF THE SEED:
THE HERITAGE OF NATURE'S INTELLIGENCE

Acharya David Frawley
(Vamadeva Shastri)

The seed can be regarded as both the root and the fruit of the entire plant. The seed is the essence of the fruit of the plant. Yet from the seed, when placed in the ground, the first roots come forth, which rely on the nutrition contained in the seed to sustain their initial growth. As they develop, these roots allow the plant to grow and to eventually mature and produce more new seeds.

The seed is therefore the beginning and the end, the origin and the completion of the whole plant. It represents the entire plant. It holds the entire cycle of life. As animals depend upon plants for their food, the seed also represents the force that feeds both the animal and human realms.

The seed carries the collective memory of the species that it represents, including the specifics of its modes of adaptation. The seed is a manifestation of nature's intelligence and carries the wisdom and the *prana*

The seed carries the collective memory of the species that it represents, including the specifics of its modes of adaptation.

(life force) of the Earth. Each seed holds the Earth within itself and is a mirror of the entire planet, its development and its evolution. We must care for the seed and plant it in the Earth for it to grow. To nourish the seed we must nourish the soil and the Earth itself.

Seeds contain many important powers of both nutrition and healing. They help sustain the seed or essence within us, the reproductive power in creatures. They aid in the development of knowledge and culture in human beings, with a special nourishing affect upon the brain and the nervous system.

Preserving and protecting the seed in nature, therefore, is the key to preserving and promoting nature as a whole. The seed is nature's legacy, her sacred record that will be passed to many generations yet to come. Diversity is the power and beauty of life, which is stifled by uniformity. The diversity of nature's seeds is also central to sustaining the diversity of nature.

The plant exists not only in the outer world of nature, but also in the inner world of our own psyche. The seed within us is our own soul or essence, our core consciousness within the heart. It carries our karmic legacy from one birth to another. We arise from this seed of awareness, dwell in it during life, and return to it at death.

The seed is a symbol of both nature's bounty and its fragility. The seed holds the potential abundance of nature in the diversity arising from its growth. Yet in its small, if not tiny, size the seed shows the fragility of nature as well. If these small seeds are altered or destroyed, a great portion of nature is lost, along with many years of natural growth, adaptation, and evolution.

Honoring the seed of the plant as sacred is the key to honoring and respecting the entire botanical kingdom, extending to honoring animal life and human life. This is our way of renewal for the future, without which the quality of our lives is likely to deteriorate.

THE INTERBREATH OF LIFE
AND THE SEEDS IT SCATTERS
'ROUND OUR PLANET

Rabbi Arthur Waskow

There are two roots in Torah from which we might draw deep caution about mixing the genes of different plants and animals today.

One is at Leviticus 19:19, part of what is called today the Holiness Code: "You shall not mate your cattle in two-kinds; you are not to sow your field with two-kinds [of seed]; you are not to put on clothing that is a mixture of two-kinds [of cloth]."

To fully understand these teachings that to a modern ear may seem quite strange, we have to notice and explore what may seem like a detour: These teachings immediately follow "Love your neighbor as yourself; *Anokhi YHWH.*"

This verse of "Love!" is central to the Torah, said Hillel the Elder, one of the greatest of the Rabbis, and his slightly younger colleague, Rabbi Jesus of Nazareth. Is it a command to love, or perhaps a statement of the truth that the way and degree with which you love your neighbor will inevitably become the way in which you love (or fail to love) yourself?

In one breath, all human beings are beloved. In the next breath, every species of plant and animal is sacred in its distinctiveness. And what connects these is the Breath of Life Itself.

And connecting this teaching about Love with the teaching to separate the seeds and semen of the different species are the two words "*Anokhi YHWH*," the two words that also begin the Revelation at Sinai.

What are these two words?

"*Anokhi*" is a Hebrew word for "I"—but not the ordinary "I" of "ego," which in Hebrew is "*Ani.*" "*Anokhi*" is the word for an exalted "I"—the entire universe and every creature in it lifted, deepened, broadened to an awesome "I."

And God's Name, the word "YHWH" that follows, is not "Yahweh," or "Jehovah," let alone "Lord" or its predecessors "*Adonai, Kyrie, Dominus.*"

For it had no vowels, and the command that grew up to forbid pronouncing it and instead to use those other words were a way of noticing that there is no way to pronounce it. Except one, and that is not what we usually call "pronouncing."

Try: "YyyyHhhhWwwwHhhh." Breathing. Try understanding it to mean "the Breathing-Spirit of all life." The Interbreath through which we breathe in what the trees breathe out, and the trees breathe in what we breathe out.

What is at stake here? In one breath, all human beings are beloved. In the next breath, every species of plant and animal is sacred in its distinctiveness. And what connects these is the Breath of Life Itself, the Awesome "I" that sees and is seen by the entire universe, the Awesome "I" in which we breathe each other, feed each other, sow each other, reap each other, fecundate each other.

To do all that, the Torah understood, we need an eco-system in which each species is unique. For the honeybee to fertilize the flower, they need to be distinct.

Yet as the centuries passed, farmers and Rabbis grew aware that species could be changed through deliberate seed-selection. The Rabbis ruled that garden lettuce and wild lettuce, leek and wild leek, even turnips and radishes, cabbage and cauliflower, were not forbidden to plant with each other as "mixtures." (*Mishna Zera'im* [Seeds], section *Kil'ayim* [Mixtures], ch 1, Mishnayot 1 and 2. In the Soncino translation, p. 87.)

Does their support for this slow evolutionary process justify the swift and urgent manipulation of the genetic substrate of hundreds of species today? I do not think so. Centuries provide their own checks and balances. Dead-ends in evolution die out indeed, and cause few deaths of humans or other life-forms as they prove themselves not able to survive. But sudden world-wide transformations are more likely to shatter ecosystems than to enrich them.

And here is where the ancient Rabbis may, despite all the limits on their scientific knowledge, have glimpsed the truth of planetary danger.

They asked what misdeed brought on the fabled Flood that drowned the web of life on Earth.

The Rabbis answered that before the Flood, all the species were mixing the water of their seed, their semen, with each other. This water washed away all biological boundaries, confounding the clarity of God's creation; so God sent a Flood of water to wash away all boundaries. (Midrash Rabbah on Bereshit 28:8; in Soncino translation, I: 228–229.)

Today we know that few species can mix together and propagate in this way. But we have also invented "genetic recombination," by which indeed the genes of one species can be introduced inside the DNA of another. Should we take the fantasy of the Rabbis as a warning to explore this new technology with the greatest care, if at all, lest we bring upon ourselves a global disaster?

Whether or not we smile at the ancient fable of the Flood, whether or not we follow the ancient regimen of separating crops, there is a wisdom communicated across millennia that warns us. The ecosystems of our planet are rich and manifold, but faced with the hypertech manipulations of today, they may be vulnerable. Take care! Breathe easy! Pause to look around us, before we plunge across the precipice.

THE REJUVENATING POWER OF SEEDS

Chief Tamale Bwoya

A seed is the mother of life on which all creatures depend. The sacredness of the seed invokes the source of life and reminds us of the mystical aspect of nature. A seed enables man to understand the purpose of his existence and the interconnection between the living and non-living.

Around Lake Victoria in East Africa, there are sacred mountains that over time set themselves on fire to rejuvenate. They burn for several months destroying all creatures thereon. When the mountains finally cool, seeds take the lead in restoring life; the same happens in volcanic formations. This process is an instinctive self-propagation and rejuvenation of planet Earth.

In African spirituality, traditional rituals reject the use of hybrids—birds, animals, or plants—because nature does not identify with them. Any hybrid or genetic modification has a weakened ability to support and sustain life at the physical and spiritual levels because biotechnology removes the essential components of natural life. In addition, creatures that feed on hybrid products gradually lose their natural character, sacredness, and connectivity to life. In short, "Man's purpose of existence is conditional: he has a right to live, but no right to manipulate life."

71

During deep contemplation on the "sacred seed" theme, nature indicated to me that the life force of living things emits from the core of the Earth. This force, radiating from the interior, eventually manifests in space and then transforms into matter; it manages, regulates, and authorizes reproduction of all living creatures on this planet. Spiritual energy from the sun facilitates the growth process of all living things, especially seeds. When a seed's growth cycle on the Earth's surface comes to an end, its material existence dissolves and the energy is committed once again to the Earth's core.

In 2012, during an international gathering of religious and spiritual leaders in Laikipia, Kenya, I received a vision indicating that humanity would face extinction. The revelation shared that our negative human actions, like seed modification, weaken ecological integrity and the natural ability for the Earth to sustain life. Later that year, during private ritual prayers with the quest to know the cause of the possible extinction, a voice similar to the one that transmitted the spiritual vision in Laikipia spoke and said, "GENETIC ENGINEERING."

I share these personal experiences to communicate the urgency of our time. The challenge before us is how to save, preserve, and keep the natural genetic heritage of all indigenous species. The spiritual chiefs and leaders globally have a role to lead the crusade to save the sacred seed because "The world was put in the hands of the chiefs" (Revelation at Laikipia).

We need to set up self-regulatory spiritual institutions not based on our previous understanding of life, but rather to monitor, evaluate, and give nature a chance to speak out.

OUR GREAT LITTLE RELATIVES–SEEDS!

Rev. Doju Dinajara Freire

Considering the interconnection between the multitude of living forms on our Mother Planet, seeds are one of the most sacred aspects of life and one of its most special expressions. In accordance with the cosmos, seeds preserve and convey the sacredness that differentiates itself among thousands of interdependent forms.

Even the smallest seed holds the power of Nature which, through plants, oxygenates the planet's atmosphere, nourishes living beings, provides medicines, perfumes, shelters, shade, and for us human beings, even fibers to be woven, and more. The preciousness of seeds in their wonderful synthesis of life makes them worthy of great respect.

With their ancient and inherent memory of life, seeds possess and show us many virtues. They have the ability to wait for the right moment to move, as great masters of patience; they know how to soften and welcome the necessary light and heat to evolve themselves, as wise teachers of life. Seeds know how to softly open, as gentle lovers in love; they know how to silently work in harmony and total gratitude, as humble spiritual masters. They know how to create beauty and strength, as only true artists can do; nothing can stop their expression, they root, grow, bloom, bear fruit, generously expressing and conveying vitality. They are like Mother Nature's milk drops whose essence benefits all life.

Even the smallest seed holds the power of Nature.

Since ancient times the vegetable seeds have been recognized by humans as great allies. For many thousands of years they have been collected, carefully stored, and planted with wisdom and harmony. From Nature we have learned how important seeds are, worthy of the sacredness of the life they carry. For many thousands of years, humans have been aware of the fact that our evolution depended on the seed's gift of life. In balance with the mystery of life, through the seeds we plant, we feed ourselves, our elderly, our children, and even the animals we have a more direct relationship with.

Currently, however, human greed generated from ignoring the sanctity of the interconnection between all of us and the environment is damaging our primordial relationship of respect towards Nature. Today our ability to interact harmoniously with the Earth—for the benefit of the planet and the future of our species—is really at risk. But we can still regain our relationship with seeds by reawakening the same ancient wisdom and the sense of the sacred that we recognized in them, that is a sense of deep respect for life in its many different forms.

All of us are as seeds; we are their children; everyone in the service of unconditional love that gives life to life. Now it is really time to remember, before it is too late for them and for us, the ancient sacred relationship with our great little relatives—seeds!

THE SEED AND THE TAO

Nan Lu, OMD

The Chinese language is a multidimensional one. Words are pictures with many layers of meaning. Interestingly, the Chinese character for seed is "zi." It also means children or "offspring"—an allusion to seeds as a sign of fertility. The seminal philosopher-teachers and spiritual leaders

who helped shape the Chinese culture used the word "zi" or seed with their names. Perhaps the best known were Lao Zi (Lao Tzu) and Zhuang Zi (or Chuang Tzu). Even Confucius was known as Kong Fu Zi or Master Teacher. These individuals and others used "zi" with their names to signify the potentiality and power of a tiny seed. There was also another reason.

In Taoist philosophy, the highest achievement is cultivating one's self to become like a child. Why? Because a child is innocent; a child has an open mind and remains alive to all the possibilities and opportunities this reality offers. In nature, one tiny seed also contains all the energetic possibilities and opportunities of Life. When humans began cultivating seeds—wheat, rice, corn, beans, flowers—and consuming their bounty, lives grew longer. Natural food contains the spirit of Life, and its energetic message of unconditional Universal love is passed through this connection to individuals who are open enough to receive it.

One of the most profound principles of the Taoist worldview is Yin-Yang. The simple black and white symbol captures the entire workings of our reality in one elegant symbol. It tells us that everything has a positive and negative energy that are designed to work in harmony; these are interrelated, inseparable, and complementary and carry power and information. Taoist philosophy also helps us understand that everything is connected. Underlying the world we experience with our five senses is the invisible world of oneness. Thousands of years ago, great masters recognized and experienced this inseparability through deep spiritual practice. They understood everything is connected through Qi or what we now call the energy field, something quantum physicists are exploring today, many thousands of years later. When you use the sacred seed to connect to Nature, you connect to Life.

Today, we approach the seed for business reasons or for personal interest. We often try to manipulate seeds for money or "science," or other reasons. Our ego makes us think we can manipulate nature and consequently Life. Nature, however, is not just a tiny seed by itself; it's connected to everything, including the soil, water, weather, and more. The manipulation of seeds, in genetically modified organisms (GMOs), for example, is the result of our limited perspective on Nature. As we continue to manipulate our precious seeds, man seeks to manipulate Life's message or the energetic frequency within them. Eventually, these actions will impact our own life and health by creating a condition of internal imbalance. If your body is already out of balance, as most individuals' bodies are in our stressed-out Western culture, eating GMO foods will only make it more so. Today, we are seeing children with more health conditions than ever before—from asthma to diabetes to obesity. Why is that? The results are cumulative. As children eat more unnaturally processed foods and unnatural things like GMO foods, an unnatural result begins to accumulate. Today's lifestyle is far more complicated than that of the ancient Taoist philosophers. It is not easy to keep balanced healthwise; so small problems can easily trigger larger ones.

When you use the sacred seed to connect to Nature, you connect to Life.

If this sounds hopeless, we have to remember that there are no accidents at the spiritual level. Everything happens for a reason; everything happens ultimately for good. The question is whether we change our angle to see the good. My Master reminds me—as I remind my Qigong students—that the answer is always within. At the spiritual level, there is no time or space; there is no judgment; there is no good or bad. The past, present, and future exist simultaneously. Positive and negative also exist at the same time—complementary, interpenetrating energy frequencies that cannot be separated—opposite sides of the same coin. We can focus on the negative side, or the positive side. We may say there's no positive side to unnatural seeds, but according to Yin-Yang theory, that's not accurate. Just because we can't see it, doesn't mean it doesn't exist.

Everything is in God's will (or whatever word one uses to refer to the indescribable unconditional love of the Universal force). From this angle, even unnatural foods are God's manifestation. In God's eye there is no time, so the answer to being able to process GMO foods may exist one thousand years from now. Also, if these foods can grow in this dimension, somehow they connect to its life force. Modern science helps us see that each cell contains a positive and negative charge, just like the Yin-Yang symbol. At the cellular level our bodies have the expertise to deal with unnatural foods from unnatural seeds, but to do this, we have to meet the requirement of cultivating a peaceful mind. We have to have faith in Nature; we have to have faith in God's creation. On the spiritual level, our body knows how to deal with unnatural foods without harming ourselves. On the physical level, the body is born with the wisdom to discover the answers within and the skill to heal itself. Our own DNA knows how to process unnatural material, if we're peaceful and have faith. If you can do this, then you will be one of those people who will discover the answers within, and then your peaceful mind will impact others. Honor the seed, and remember to honor the wisdom you were born with. You, too, are in God's will.

THE PARABLE OF THE SOWER

Rev. Richard Cizik

To the followers of Jesus, the Parable of the Sower is well known. In it, a farmer goes out to the field to sow seed, and finds that as he scatters the seed it falls on different kinds of ground.

Rocky soil, beaten paths, thorn bushes—the farmer must sow in spite of the conditions of the fields. And a good bit of seed falls on good soil and eventually produces crops of various yields.

So the same seed produces no crops, some crops, or a great crop. Jesus warns his listeners, "He who has ears, let him hear." Of course, everyone has ears. But this will take more than ordinary listening to understand. Metaphors require not just to see but to behold in a new way. A mystery is being revealed.

The "seed" can be variously understood as the "Word," written or living, the Word of God that transforms our lives, or the Living Word, Jesus himself. What matters most is what we do with this Truth.

A radical reversal is required. From Genesis to Revelation, we are instructed to be caretakers and stewards of the Earth. But we as people of faith, especially Christians, have not done this. The Truth has fallen on barren land, or been choked out by the weeds of production and consumption, consumerism, and materialism.

We have been seduced into thinking the land belongs to us, instead of God. Justice and righteousness are at stake. A great violation has taken place.

We have substituted a "take, make, and waste" mentality (take from the Earth, make things, and put the waste back into the Earth) for what was intended—to simply borrow from the Earth, use its resources, and then replenish the land.

Instead we pursue a destiny fraught with danger. Our reliance on fossil fuels destroys the planet, and we are left to wonder if we aren't the ones being destroyed. That is, if we have ears to hear and eyes to see. Most of our fellow human beings do not; they are oblivious to the carnage.

God says, "I will destroy those who destroy the earth" (Revelation 11:18). Is what is happening God or is it really us? Are we not doing it to ourselves? The law of sowing and reaping is immutable. We are reaping in our bodies what we have sown, namely toxins, chemicals, plasticides, and carcinogens.

A faith the size of a mustard seed is enough to begin the Great Reversal of this scandal. Repentance happens. Healing of the land occurs. Fear becomes hope. Lament is turned to joy. Death is turned to life.

The unending story of each generation is whether it will obey the command—to care for the land. A new consciousness is required. A new narrative written. It must not be rejected, spiritualized, or sacramentalized.

It is now our story. A tiny seed that will flourish and take over the world!

THE SECRET OF THE SEED

Sraddhalu Ranade

It is said that the tree lies waiting in the seed, and when the circumstances are right, it grows out and reveals itself in the world. This is obvious for all to see and verify. What is not obvious is how an entire massive and gigantic tree can hide within this tiny fragile seed that was itself once a piece and a fragment of its parent tree.

The heart wonders at this marvel and feels the presence of the Sacred in the seed and its unfolding. The mind too is touched by the sense of the Sacred, but it responds differently—it is drawn to explore the mystery and reveal its secrets to our sight even at the risk of profaning the miraculous. The mind pursues relentlessly peeling off the layers of Phenomenon that veil, digging deeper into forms and structures, hoping to find at the heart of the mysterious and magical a single mathematical formula, an incantation or law that will explain it all. It studies the cells, molecules, genes, and DNA; it maps out biochemical reactions, protein folding, spontaneous yet coordinated complex chain reactions, and electric fields that align and govern them. Yet, when all is said and done, when the enormously complex machinery of the cells and seed is described and codified, nothing is really explained and the secret remains even more deeply hidden!

The mystery remains, seemingly more revealed to our understanding, but in fact even more deeply hidden. For, the massive store of scientific knowledge conceals even more thoroughly the source and purpose of it all! Every layer of knowledge studied, peeled off, and documented, reveals more miracles, more puzzles, and raises even more questions. What seemed at first to be reducible to a single formula or law, is now broken into many fields of specialization, each becoming a world unto itself, each separating from others more and more, as it narrows its focus upon less and less. Specializations give way to super-specializations, disciplines separate and rejoin in inter-disciplinary explorations. Before we know it, we realise we have begun to study the entire universe through the lens of a single Seed!

Therein lies the secret of the seed—it is in fact the whole world enfolding itself, condensed into a Seed. Just as the world is not merely the machinery of molecules and atoms driven by blind mechanical laws, so too the seed is not merely biochemical machinery driven by a bundle of DNA codes. Even as the world is in truth a great Energy pouring itself through rhythms and unfolding into patterns of beauty, so too is the Seed the compact form of a mighty Force. The seed can reshape its environment and bring forth out of dead, inert, and resistant stone the gigantic and graceful, living, growing tree that bursts out into millions of flowers of the subtlest fragrances, each unique in form and grace, none ever repeated! As the secret of the world lies in the Intent and Purpose of its manifestation, so the secret of the seed lies in the Idea of the Tree that drives its overt molecular machinery and guides it flawlessly at each step to assert and fulfill itself in the world.

The Seed-Idea pre-exists, and survives the destruction of the form and machinery of the seed. It lives before the tree was born and was the cause of the tree's appearance. Free of form and machinery, it lives in each branch and leaf and flower of the tree, entirely present in each cell, and therefore also in each new seed that forms out of its parent tree. It contains within it all knowledge of its own development: it knows how to deal with all circumstances, each challenge and opposition that the soil, water, air, and light may throw at it in the whole Universe; it knows also how to balance and realign the conflicting energies of Nature and redirect them to fulfill its own purpose; it seizes on the randomness and chaotic play of Nature's powers and forces and compels them to take on forms of an evolving order, harmony, and beauty.

It is the Seed-Idea hiding in the heart of the seed that brings Order out of Chaos, dealing with exact knowledge and power precisely measured at each step through the machinery of the seed. Its omniscience knows its right relation with all things in the Universe; its omnipotence can master all energies that impinge upon it; its omnipresence supports every seed with the same sense of purpose wherever it may be planted in the Universe, each growing uniquely in its unique circumstances.

The secret of the Seed is not a formula or law of Nature; it is Seed-Idea, omniscient, omnipotent, and omnipresent timelessly in eternity. The secret of the Seed is the Divine Himself conceiving the Idea of the Tree and incarnating Himself using the form and machinery of the seed to fulfill Himself in the world. All things in the universe therefore emerge from a seed—whether atom or molecule or plant or animal or human. The Universe itself bursts out from the Seed in a Big Bang when the Divine conceives Himself as the universe. All is Himself cast out into innumerable forms in infinite variations playing out infinite possibilities. The Seed is His hiding place from where He emerges to reveal Himself uniquely, and into which He withdraws to hide once again in His *Lila*, the eternal Play of hide-and-seek.

SEEDS ARE THE TRANSCENDENT STUFF OF LIFE

Blu Greenberg

It was from a young boy that I learned about the transcendent nature of seeds. I was working on a graduate school paper, the hypothesis of which was that Orthodox Jews believed in the existence of God in the universe. Of course, my respondents, thirty random members of my synagogue, affirmed this as an article of faith; but when it came time for proof or certainty, there was plenty of equivocation. Only one person, the cantor of the synagogue whose heartfelt prayer had led the community for almost three dozen years, had no doubts whatsoever. God was his intimate father, present in his life every single day, all day. One evening, still curious about the other twenty-nine religious souls, men and women who carefully observed the commandments attendant to an orthodox way of life, I returned home to find my ten-year-old son waiting for some conversation. I decided to test out the God questions on him. "Of course there is a God," JJ answered. He went on to offer his proof. "You see those cucumbers? Well, one tiny seed becomes a cucumber, and another tiny seed grows into a tomato, and another becomes a banana. Someone is making that happen. Someone is making the difference. That someone must be God."

Without using those words, JJ was talking about the DNA of a seed—the brilliant key to the universe in a speck of an object. What JJ was saying was that God's intelligence and power are encompassed in a single seed, a specially marked, carefully programmed unit, all the more remarkable because of its infinitesimal size.

And it is not just DNA. Seeds are the transcendent stuff of life, for so much about our lives comes from seeds. Seeds are what enabled life to be maintained from primitive times unto today: every human being ever born came from a seed; so too, all animal and plant life that sustained us as food, all that humans wore on their backs before synthetics, all aspects of shelter from the excesses of nature, all original tools of culture such as writing, music, and art—indeed everything that we depended on to continue the generations.

Given the importance of seed, it is not unfair to say that in our everyday lives we tend to take for granted their power and importance. We discard seeds as garbage without a thought of the mysteries they hold; we pay more for watermelons and lemons engineered to be free of those pesky things.

Judaism partially compensates in acknowledging the masterminding ability of seeds in their end product, as my son did. Among my favorite aspects of Judaism are the blessings we recite during the course of each day, blessings over the wonders of nature—food, natural events such as thunder and lightning and great oceans, scenes of beauty, persons of great wisdom, changes of seasons, and more. Interestingly, as regards the blessings over food, we are taught to recite not one global blessing for all food but differentiated formulations of thanks to God. Before biting into an apple, we recite a blessing

Seeds are the transcendent stuff of life, for so much about our lives comes from seeds.

on this fruit that grows on a tree; we recite a different blessing on a cucumber that grows in the ground or a grape that comes from a vine or bread that comes from a wheat stalk in the earth. It is not the fullest recognition of the brilliance of seed, but it does heighten awareness that nature is an exquisitely designed, variegated entity that connects us to the Divine.

JJ's life was taken a dozen years ago, at age thirty-six, in a bicycle accident. I never think of seed without thinking of God, and of JJ.

THE STUNTED SEED

Teny Pirri-Simonian

The "sacred seed" is God's gift to humanity. Poverty and economic injustice are evidence of the mismanagement of this gift.

In the biblical narrative of creation, God orders all animals and herbs to become 'fruitful and multiply' through their seeds. He then creates men and women in His own 'image' and 'likeness' and delegates to them the responsibility of taking care of His creation (Genesis 1).

In Christianity the Divine participated in human life through the incarnation of Jesus Christ. Jesus taught the mutuality of love and the right relationship with God, other human beings, and the environment. In his parables Jesus speaks of the seed and its sacred quality as an essential resource that both breeds its own kind and feeds the birds of the air (Matthew 13:4). Because the presence of the Divine in all of creation attaches a spiritual meaning to life, moral judgments should not differentiate "quality of life" from "sanctity of life." God's free gift of life demands responsible management of creation and the just distribution of its fruits.

The "sacred seed" is God's gift to humanity.

Market forces and the political and economic interests of those in power are destroying the abundant gift of seeds that God provided for responsible production and consumption. Currently, in many parts of the world, people have become irresponsible consumers, and seeds are no longer assets for the average farmer. Many countries and nations can no longer control the success of their economic and social development programs because of globalization and growing interdependence.

Today, particularly in poor countries, transnational business organizations dictate what sort of food will be consumed and the nutritional value of that food. These enterprises seek to maximize the production of crops for export by forcing small farmers to give up their indigenous life-giving agriculture and buy genetically modified seeds for higher yields. Human dignity is being sacrificed as God's economy of creation and distributive justice is replaced by an economy of greed and the accumulation of wealth by the few. How far should enterprises be allowed to manipulate the cycle of the "sacred seed" and transform it into a dead-end "stunted seed," thereby destroying the 'image' of the human person created in the 'likeness' of God? This situation is a challenge to spiritual communities and they are called to respond!

THE SEED-ING OF CONSCIOUSNESS, SEED-ING OF THE HEART

Tiokasin Ghosthorse

"The intuitive mind is a sacred gift and the rational mind is a faithful servant. We have created a society that honors the servant and has forgotten the gift."
—Albert Einstein

We humans often perceive plants, animals, birds, and other life-forms as lacking consciousness, relegating them to primal instinct.

It is not so.

A *Seed-ing* has consciousness, a need to sustain life, and an intuitive relationship with other life-forms excluding human explanations of lofty science. We say something has to think, feel, or have awareness of the world around itself to have any value for humans. We cheat ourselves as a species when arrogance dictates reason and thus misunderstands the *seed-ing*, making relational-intuition tedious.

Heart-think is listening to our intuition, recognizing the immature thoughts of emotional reactions, which diminish the urgency to act responsibly towards Mother Earth.

Nasula (naw-soo-lah) is a Lakota word metaphorically meaning the *brain* (head) is purely a *seed-ing* of the *heart*.

The first thought was the first *seed-ing* of creation. What we do in planting and cultivating seeds are first thoughts. When a person wakes with seeds of thought, creation, action, remedy, healing, nourishment, generosity, appreciation, and intelligence, it is one word—*Nasula*. The word in simpler terms means your brain (head), thoughts, eyes, ears, nose, voice, and taste (instinctuals). It is a "seed of the heart" (intuitionals) and the *heart* changes instinctual elements into intuition—a *seed-ing*.

We understand the metaphorical *seed* has physical thought of potential, one of reality without deficiency.

The *Heart* emanates electromagnetic fields according to feelings or *heart-think* and extends outside of the body. It is 100,000 times electrically stronger and 5,000 times magnetically stronger than the brain. As a *seed-ing* in the womb the heart evolves, beats, and synchronizes the mother's brainwaves to her baby's heartbeat, before the brain is created. The brain receives more information from the heart than it sends to the heart, and 60 to 65 percent of heart cells are neural (brain) cells, including temporary and enduring memories of intuitive experiences.

Heart-think is listening to our intuition, recognizing the immature thoughts of emotional reactions, which diminish the urgency to act responsibly towards Mother Earth. She is a *relationship* consisting of thoughts, neurons, memories, and information evolving from the heart— *Nasula*. We no longer speak a *heart-think* language, because western education teaches that the brain is the center and thus we speak only a *brain-think* language.

Nasula includes realities of the physical world, where the sun rises and sets, and the four seasons teach our young ones about "living reality," not based on myth or solely on scientific *brain-think* that "uses reality" only for humans.

In 1930, Einstein observed that, "Among all people, twelve-year-old (Hopi) children were probably the best prepared to grasp his Theory of Relativity." If all Native peoples of the western hemisphere were introduced to him, he would have found among them the Theory of Relativity being lived as the *seed-ing* "sacred gift."

We must *Seed* a Mother Earth *Spring* movement and ready our *Nasula*. Mother Earth is not a noun.

Mitakuye Oyasin (All My Relations)

SEEDS AND THE COSMIC SEEDING OF ONENESS

Sufi Rehman Muhaiyaddeen

The huge cosmic system is comprised of diverse universal phenomena organized in meticulous formations to perform certain functions in which individual performances influence the performances of their respective systems and thereby help in achieving their individual as well as collective objectives.

The creatures of the Almighty exist in a variety of life-forms on the planet Earth. They are part of us, and we are part of them in the divine scheme of

Seeds are not a human invention, but rather represent millions of years of biological evolution.

biodiversity. According to the divine format, the number of species of plants, animals, and microorganisms within their enormous diversity of genes, along with the different ecosystems on the planet, such as deserts, rainforests, and coral reefs, have preserved planetary life in such a way that they support one another and enable the rest of the life-forms to sustain and evolve. In this regard each natural seeding is precious and every seed is sacred because of the indispensable role they play in Nature.

In the modern age of commercialism we have been introduced to the concept of 'Bio Nullius,' or empty life, on which anyone can claim "intellectual property rights." Claiming rights on seeds, biodiversity, and life-forms is the result of such an unrealistic approach. In reality, Nature has deep interconnectedness and is not empty. Seeds are not a human invention, but rather represent millions of years of biological evolution.

By tampering with seeds for commercial gain and to claim property rights for profit, biotechnology companies are both tampering with nature and also depriving farmers of their divine right of preservation. The rapid loss of crop diversity due to this practice during the past century is one of many evidences of its crucial outcome.

The initiative by Dr. Vandana Shiva to create the book *Sacred Seed* is a substantial step forward in combining religious and spiritual voices for the preservation of Nature.

THE LANGUAGE OF THE SEED

Anat Vaughan-Lee

A root definition of the word "seed" is the active verb, to sow. In our daily language we also use the word seed as a metaphor to describe new beginnings, new ideas, a sense of purpose and hope. However the true and sacred source and meaning of this word has been censored from us, forgotten, uncelebrated.

In our Western culture we have been accustomed to process knowledge, scientific knowledge, based upon left-brain analytic thinking. We are exposed to a world that predominantly operates by masculine values, and thus our thoughts and language have taken this form, cutting us off from the wholeness which belongs to the language of life, life in its wonder and eternal rebirth. This is the language of the seed.

Like breath so is the seed. Given. It is an inseparable part of our self and our environment. The seed holds a very great secret—it never gets old. It is the eternal YES to life. The power of a tiny seed is unimaginable. It is the force of promise, the covenant of life, the agent of return. It is the ever-present mystery of giving.

Within it lies the mystery of time, with its cycle of the seasons and of death and rebirth. It possesses both masculine and feminine qualities, which are in constant creative dialogue. From the dark womb of the feminine the direct force of the masculine emerges and shoots up into the light. Light and dark are in constant relationship. The seed is also both the center and the circumference, calling us to remember the sacred nature of life, the interconnected language of the universe, a song of oneness communicating to us and telling us, again and again, that we too are partaking in a primordial love affair, a union of masculine and feminine.

The seed holds a very great secret—it never gets old. It is the eternal YES to life.

When we begin to realize this, a very mysterious process is awakened within us. We begin to participate in the great mystery of being that is so central to our existence.

Returning to the language of the seed is a returning to the language of life, no longer from a place of separation but from a place of sacred communion. It is the language of remembrance. When we hold this awareness within our body we become a full participant with the Earth and the cosmos—at that moment something is allowed to live according to its true nature. That which is remembered lives. When we hold this consciousness in our heart, we naturally offer it back to life. This not only gives life meaning, but like a seed it revitalizes it. We then participate not only in the mystery of our own being but in the whole wonder of creation.

COSMIC ECOLOGY AND DIVERSITY:
LESSONS FROM THE VEDAS

Swamini Svatmavidyananda

In the vision of the Vedas, there is only one presence, one source, known as Brahman, which is limitless and all-pervasive, invoked as the creator and the truth of the self. We have never been preoccupied with this one-God-many-Gods business. For us, there is only God. The air we breathe, the light of the sun, oceans, rivers, mountains and forests, seeds and plants—are all manifestations of Brahman, God. Therefore, every atom of this creation is sacred.

Unlike certain theologies that tout human dominion over nature, over the "soulless" world of animals and plants, in the Hindu tradition, the relationship advocated between humans and the natural world is one of harmonic inter-dependence, whose guiding tenet is *ahimsa*, non-injury. The Vedas, which reveal the interconnectedness of everything, teach us to revere all life-forms by doing our part in pre-serving this creation. The Vedas and the Bhagavad Gita consider the need to care for one's natural habitat as a moral imperative of one's being, and a unique opportunity for one's spiritual growth. Since everything in creation is interconnected, the well-being of our surroundings is inextricably connected to our own well-being. The Bhagavad Gita says that anyone who refrains from participating in the sacred reciprocity of caring is to be considered as a thief who disrupts the cosmic equilibrium for the sake of his/her own pleasure and consumption, and whose life, therefore, is a burden on Mother Earth.

These timeless and universal tenets of non-injury and reverence for all things are extremely pertinent for the contemporary world where diversity has been beheaded at the altar of homogenization, leading to the ascent of a dangerous monoculture that is fast eclipsing all aspects of life, from the diet we ingest to the deities we invoke. This has led to a growing disconnect between humans and nature, a separation that we can no longer afford to feed.

The air we breathe, the light of the sun, oceans, rivers, mountains and forests, seeds and plants—are all manifestations of Brahman, God. Therefore, every atom of this creation is sacred.

In this regard, the desecration of the seed by agribusinesses such as Monsanto has become a metaphor for disrupting the most subtle and sacred of nature's bounty—the gift of diversity. Manipulating the seed that represents biodiversity to conform to the profit demands of a reigning monoculture has dire consequences for our ecosystem, which includes our bodies and minds. The seed represents the storehouse of knowledge and diversity and contains the blueprint of life on Earth. Extreme genetic engineering, leading to "terminator seeds," making them incapable of reproduction, is a rank example of self-sabotage. In sowing such seeds, we are sowing land mines that will one day erupt into a raging cacophony of dissonance, destroying everything in its wake, causing pathologies too deviant to reverse. When we violate ecological laws, we have to bear the brunt of the consequences of our actions.

Before we become deaf-mute spectators to the inevitable chain of events that will seal the fate of the future generations of life as we know it, let us together heed the timeless call of the collective wisdom of ancient cultures that speak the common tongue of oneness and compassion, of diversity and mutual interdependence. In so doing, we participate in the steady flow of a cosmic ecology of reciprocity and sacred exchange. Such a lifestyle expresses itself by celebrating diversity at all levels—religious, cultural, and biodiversity. This is the best defense against the tyrannical reign of monopolizing cultures.

CONTRIBUTORS

Foreword
Dena Merriam
Founder and Convener, Global Peace Initiative of Women

Ms. Merriam began working in the interfaith movement in the late 1990s when she served as Vice Chair of the Millennium World Peace Summit of Religious and Spiritual Leaders held at the United Nations in New York. She subsequently convened a meeting of women religious and spiritual leaders at the Palais des Nations in Geneva and from that gathering founded the Global Peace Initiative of Women (GPIW) in 2002, an organization chaired by a multi-faith group of women spiritual leaders. Under the leadership of women, the mission of this organization is to enable women, men, and young adults to facilitate healing and reconciliation in areas of conflict and post-conflict, and to bring spiritual resources to help address critical global problems. In 2008 Ms. Merriam was one of the founding members of the Contemplative Alliance, which focuses on the collective inner work needed for the positive transformation of the global society. Ms. Merriam received her Master's Degree from Columbia University. She is a long-time student of the Indian Master Paramahansa Yogananda and a practitioner of Kriya Yoga.

www.gpiw.org

Introduction
Vandana Shiva

Dr. Vandana Shiva was trained as a physicist and did her Ph.D. on "Hidden Variables and Non-locality in Quantum Theory." For the past 40 years she has been active in the ecology movement. Her background in Quantum Theory and her work at the grassroots have reinforced her worldview that nothing is separable, everything is connected, that nature is not dead matter, but a self-organised living system of which we are a part. Dr. Shiva is the founder of Navdanya and the Research Foundation for Science, Technology and Ecology. She is the author of numerous books, including *Staying Alive* and *Making Peace with the Earth*. Among her many awards are the Right Livelihood Award, also called the Alternative Nobel Prize.

www.navdanya.org

Sacred Seed—The Christian Orthodox Tradition
His All Holiness, Bartholomew, Archbishop of Constantinople, New Rome and Ecumenical Patriarch

His All Holiness, Ecumenical Patriarch Bartholomew is spiritual leader to 300 million Orthodox Christians worldwide. Born in Imvros (Gokceada), Turkey (1940), he is 270th Archbishop of the 2000-year-old Church founded by St. Andrew, serving as Archbishop of Constantinople-New Rome, and Ecumenical Patriarch (since 1991). His efforts to promote human rights and religious tolerance, together with his pioneering work for international peace and environmental protection, have placed him at the forefront of global visionaries as an apostle of love, peace, and reconciliation. In 1997, he was awarded the Gold Medal of the United States Congress.
www.patriarchate.org

The Seed of Compassion
His Holiness the 17th Gyalwang Karmapa, Ogyen Trinley Dorje

His Holiness the 17th Gyalwang Karmapa, Ogyen Trinley Dorje, is the head of the 900-year-old Karma Kagyu Lineage and guide to millions of Buddhists around the world. Currently 28 years old, the Karmapa resides in his temporary home at Gyuto Monastery in India after making a dramatic escape from Tibet in the year 2000. As an environmental activist, computer enthusiast, and world spiritual leader whose teachings are often webcast live, the 17th Gyalwang Karmapa has brought the Karmapa lineage's activities fully into the 21st century.
www.kagyuoffice.org

Seeds of a New Humanity
Sister Joan Chittister, OSB

Joan Chittister is an internationally known writer and lecturer. She currently serves as co-chair of the Global Peace Initiative of Women, facilitating a worldwide network of women peacebuilders from all the faith traditions. Sister Joan is a member of the Benedictine Sisters of Erie, Pennsylvania, USA, and has written fifty books. She has received numerous awards for her work for justice, peace, and equality, especially for women in church and in society. Her latest books include, *Following the Path: The Search for a Life of Passion, Purpose and Joy* (Random House) and *Happiness* (Wm. Eerdmans). Her web column, "From Where I Stand," in the *National Catholic Reporter* is routinely

reprinted on *Huffington Post*, other websites, newsletters, and magazines. Her doctorate is from Penn State University in speech communications theory and she was an elected-fellow of St. Edmund's College, Cambridge University. Currently she is the executive director of Benetvision, a resource and research center for contemporary spirituality located in Erie. She served as prioress of the Benedictine Sisters of Erie for twelve years and recently developed the Monasteries of the Heart program, an on-line community of 5000 spiritual seekers around the world connecting to common values and springs out of the contemplative tradition.
www.benetvision.org · www.monasteriesoftheheart.org

Seeds and the Story of the Soul
Llewellyn Vaughan-Lee
Llewellyn Vaughan-Lee, Ph.D., is a Sufi teacher. Born in London in 1953, he has followed the Naqshbandi Sufi path since he was nineteen. In 1991 he became the successor of Irina Tweedie, who brought this particular Indian branch of Sufism to the West and is the author of *Daughter of Fire: A Diary of a Spiritual Training with a Sufi Master*. He then moved to Northern California and founded The Golden Sufi Center. Author of several books, he has specialized in the area of dreamwork, integrating the ancient Sufi approach to dreams with the insights of Jungian Psychology. Since 2000 his writing and teaching have been on spiritual responsibility in our present time of transition, and an awakening global consciousness of oneness. More recently he has written about the feminine, the *anima mundi* (World Soul), and spiritual ecology. His recent books are the anthology, *Spiritual Ecology: The Cry of the Earth,* and *Darkening of the Light: Witnessing the End of an Era*. He has also been featured in the TV series *Global Spirit* and was interviewed by Oprah Winfrey as a part of her *Super Soul Sunday* series.
www.goldensufi.org · www.workingwithoneness.org · www.spiritualecology.org

Seed As the Cosmic Principle
Swami Veda Bharati
Swami Veda Bharati, 81, born in a Sanskrit-speaking family, has meditated all his life since the age of four and a half; he is a renowned meditation master. He expounded the Vedas and Yoga Sutras to thousands from the age of nine. Author of more than twenty books, a poet and scholar, he holds the highest academic degrees from western

universities. He has travelled and lectured internationally for the past 67 years. Now on a five-year vow of silence, Swamiji is founder of Association of Himalayan Yoga Meditation Societies International (ahymsin@gmail.com) and founder of Swami Rama Sadhaka Grama Ashram, Rishikesh, India (sadhakagrama@gmail.com), and is also Spiritual Guide to the Ashram of late Swami Rama of the Himalayas, who initiated him into the highest meditation consciousness.
www.ahymsin.org

Seeds of Promise
Rabbi Rami Shapiro

A congregational rabbi for twenty years, Rabbi Rami currently co-directs One River Wisdom School and Holy Rascals Foundation. Rami blogs at rabbirami.blogspot.com, writes a regular column for *Spirituality and Health Magazine* called "Roadside Assistance for the Spiritual Traveler," and hosts the weekly Internet radio show, *How to Be a Holy Rascal* on Unity On-line Radio (unity.fm/program/howtobeaholyrascal.com). His newest book is *Perennial Wisdom for the Spiritually Independent* (SkyLight Paths, Sept 2013).
www.rabbirami.com · www.oneriverwisdomschool.com · www.holyrascals.com

The Seed of Love
Pir Zia Inayat-Khan

Pir Zia Inayat-Khan, Ph.D., is president of the Sufi Order International and founder of Suluk Academy. Since 2004, Pir Zia has served as Head of the Sufi Order International, guiding Sufi communities in North America, South America, Europe, the Middle East, Asia, and the South Pacific. To provide opportunities for intensive Sufi study, Pir Zia founded the Suluk Academy. Based at the Abode of the Message in upstate New York, the Suluk Academy currently offers courses for Sufi initiates in New York, California, and France. Pir Zia has taken part in numerous interreligious and interdisciplinary gatherings. To encourage such conversations and collaborations, he founded Seven Pillars House of Wisdom. Pir Zia is also a Fellow of the Lindisfarne Association, and an Advisor to the Contemplative Alliance. He is the author of *Saracen Chivalry: Counsels on Valor, Generosity and the Mystical Quest* (Suluk Press, 2012).
www.pirzia.org

A Little Seed of Awakening
Acharya Judy Lief
Acharya Judy Lief is a senior student of Venerable Chögyam Trungpa Rinpoche, who empowered her as a teacher in the Buddhist and Shambhala traditions. She has edited many of his books, including the recently published three-volume *Profound Treasury of the Ocean of Dharma*. For over thirty years she has been offering workshops and retreats on Buddhist psychology and meditation. Judy has been active in the movement to improve end-of-life care and is the author of *Making Friends with Death: A Buddhist Guide to Encountering Mortality*. She is a founding member of the Contemplative Alliance, a project of the Global Peace Initiative of Women. Judy is married and is both a mother and a grandmother.
www.judylief.com

Seed of Wisdom
Swami Atmarupananda
Swami Atmarupananda is a renowned scholar, teacher, and Monk of the Ramakrishna Order of India, a monastic organization dedicated to the teaching of Vedanta. He joined the Order in 1969 and spent many years in India engaged in monastic, scholarly, and spiritual training. He combines a contemplative and mystical approach with an extraordinary scholarly training and a good sense of humor that are helpful in explaining subtle concepts of Hinduism to Western students. He has presented in a number of international gatherings on the emergence of contemplative practice in the West and spiritual ecology led by the Global Peace Initiative of Women.
www.spiritualpaths.net/spiritual-paths-books/videos/swami-atmarupananda-interspirituality

A Haudenosaunee Reflection on "Seed: The Power of Life"
Dr. Dan Longboat, Roronhiakewen (He Clears the Sky)
Dan Longboat is Mohawk from the Six Nations of the Grand River. He is Director of the Indigenous Environmental Studies Program at Trent University, Peterborough, Ontario, Canada. Dan is known for his Traditional Haudenosaunee knowledge and has taught Mohawk culture at Trent in addition to his work in Indigenous Environmental Studies. He was the first Director of Studies of the Ph.D. program. Dan completed his Ph.D. in Environmental Studies at York University.

The Sacred Bond
Sobonfu Somé

Sobonfu Somé is a respected lecturer, activist, and author. She is one of the foremost voices of African spirituality to come to the West, bringing insights and healing gifts from her West-African culture to this one. Sobonfu often tours the United States and Europe teaching workshops. Her books include: *The Spirit of Intimacy: Ancient Teachings in the Ways of Relationships, Welcoming Spirit Home: Ancient Teachings to Celebrate Children & Community,* and *Falling Out of Grace: Meditations on Loss, Healing, and Wisdom.* She also authored the CD set, *Women's Wisdom from the Heart of Africa.* Sobonfu founded Wisdom Spring, Inc., an organization dedicated to the preservation and sharing of indigenous wisdom, and fundraises for wells, schools, and health projects in Africa. For more information about Sobonfu's projects and teaching schedule, please visit: www.sobonfu.com · www.wisdomspring.org

The Sacred Mystery of Physis: Honoring Seed in Ancient Greece
Christoph Quarch, PhD

Christoph Quarch (*1964) is a philosopher, theologian, author, and coach in the fields of philosophy and spirituality, and teaches Ethics and Cultural History at Fulda University of Applied Sciences in Germany. He has served as Ambassador of the World Wisdom Council and consultant to the Parliament of the World's Religions. Quarch was the former chief-editor of *Publik-Forum* magazine, the editor of the monthly magazine, *Evangelische Kommentare,* and he served as the Academic Director of the German Protestant Kirchentag in Fulda from 2000–2006. Quarch has published more than thirty books on philosophical and spiritual subjects, some in collaboration with spiritual leaders from diverse religions and faith traditions; he also leads a Europe-wide series of seminars and workshops on philosophy and spirituality. His current main field of interest is the actuality of ancient Greek Philosophy and Mythology. www.christophquarch.de

The Seed—The Source
Sister Jayanti

Sister Jayanti is the European Director of the Brahma Kumaris, with over forty years of experience of Raja Yoga meditation and its practical application in daily

life. Her gentle voice and profound insights on spiritual solutions to everyday problems have touched the hearts of thousands around the world.
www.brahmakumaris.org/uk/awakening

Seeds of the Spirit: A Call to Spiritual Action for Mother Earth
A Haudenosaunee Reflection
Diane Longboat

Kahontakwas (Diane) Longboat, Turtle Clan, Mohawk Nation from the Six Nations Grand River Territory, is a ceremonial leader, healer, and traditional teacher of Indigenous spiritual ways. She offers ceremonies at the Sacred Lodge of Soul of the Mother where a Sacred Fire burns for the healing of Mother Earth and the spiritual renewal of humanity. Diane also holds professional degrees in education (M.Ed.). She has spoken at universities in Canada and at many national and international conferences and gatherings on the topic of spiritual renewal and education as a determinant for nation building. From 1976 to 1994, Diane was director of research programs and educational offices both provincially and nationally with First Nations organizations and the University of Toronto. She currently consults with First Nations Governments and their organizations as well as with global organizations around the issues of sovereignty in First Nations jurisdiction over education and the role of spirituality in leading the transformative process.
www.spiritmatterscommunity.com/kahontakwas-diane-longboat
www.soulofthemother.org/OurBoard.html

Seeds and the Sacred
Mary Ann Burris

Mary Ann Burris is the founder of the Trust for Indigenous Culture and Health (TICAH) based in Kenya. Her work centers around the importance of tradition and culture in implementing health and development work, and the use of ritual and art for healing and building peace. Before moving to Kenya in 1996, Mary Ann lived and worked in China several times. From 1991 to 1995, she worked for the Ford Foundation in Beijing, China, developing their programs on reproductive health and women's rights, and from 1996 to 2003, she was responsible for building the Ford Foundation's programs in sexual and reproductive health and youth development in East Africa. Mary Ann is a member of the Ngong Sangha in Nairobi, and a participant in the Council of Elders project of the Worldwide Indigenous Science Network (WISN). She serves on several boards and is writing a meditation manual for use with children and adults in the Nairobi slum communities where TICAH works.

www.ticahealth.org

There Is No Life Without a Seed and There Is No Seed Without a Life
Venerable Bhante Buddharakkhita

Venerable Bhante Buddharakkhita was born and raised in Uganda, Africa. He first encountered Buddhism in 1990 while living in India, and he began practicing meditation in 1993. He was ordained as a Buddhist monk by the late Venerable U Silananda in 2002 at the Tathagata Meditation Center in San Jose, California, and then he spent eight years under the guidance of Bhante Gunaratana at the Bhavana Society, West Virginia. He is the founder and abbot of the Uganda Buddhist Center in Uganda. Founder and President of the Bodhi Education Foundation, a non-profit organization based in Maryland, USA, he holds other international positions such as: executive member of International Buddhist Confederation, India; International Advisory Board member of Buddhist Peace Fellowship, San Francisco, USA; an official member, World Buddhist Summit, Kobe City, Japan. Besides spending time at the Buddhist Center in Uganda, he is the spiritual director of Flowering Lotus Meditation Center in Magnolia, Mississippi. He serves on the council of spiritual advisers to the Global Buddhist Relief, New Jersey. Bhante has been teaching meditation in Africa, Australia, Europe, Asia, and the US, since 2005. His book, *Planting Dhamma Seeds: The Emergence of Buddhism in Africa*, tells the story of his religious and spiritual work in Africa.

www.ugandabuddhistcenter.org

Listening to the Hidden Heart of Seeds
Angela Fischer

Angela Fischer is the author of several books on feminine spirituality and the oneness of life, and has lead seminars and retreats since her twenties. After university studies, followed by training and work in the field of body and energy healing and the experience of organic farming in the early 1980s, living very close to nature, she met her spiritual path and teacher, and dedicated her life and work to the meaning of mystical life in the present time. Integrating her work with family life, her focus has

been on reanimating a genuine feminine spirituality, which leads to living women's spiritual responsibility for life and the Earth, as well as recovering the feminine principle in both women and men. Following the Sufi path since 1985, she provides space for people to meditate together and share questions and inspiration, with an emphasis on living the sacred in daily life. She is married, mother of four children, and lives in northern Germany.
www.einheit-des-lebens.net/englisch

And the Last Shall Be First
Shailly Barnes, Adam Barnes, Rev. Liz Theoharis, Rev. Kathy Maskell: Poverty Initiative at Union Theological Seminary, NYC

Established in 2004, the Poverty Initiative's (PI) mission is to raise up generations of grassroots religious and community leaders dedicated to building a social movement to end poverty, led by the poor. Through three national truth commissions, two leadership schools, nine strategic dialogues, four books, dozens of poverty immersions and seminar courses, and numerous events and exchanges with global grassroots leaders, PI has established a wide and deep network spanning 28 states and 17 countries. Over these ten years, PI has steadfastly maintained that the contradiction of poverty in contemporary US society is both a violation of human rights and a central focus of theological study. In November 2013, PI joined Kairos, the Center for Religions, Rights and Social Justice, as its cornerstone program.
www.povertyinitiative.org · www.kairoscenter.org

Seeds and the Miracle of Life
Aliaa Rafea, PhD

Aliaa R. Rafea is a professor of Anthropology at Ain Shams University, Women's College. She makes use of anthropological perspectives to understanding issues related to religion, politics, and culture. Founder and chair of The Human Foundation, Professor Rafea wrote book chapters that were published in India, Japan, Morocco, Canada, and USA, and numerous academic articles. Author and co-author of several books, among which is *The Root of All Evil: An Exposition to Prejudice, Fundamentalism and Gender Bias* (2007), she shared in editing and wrote a chapter in *A Force Such as the World has Never Known: Women Changing the World* (2013). An expert for the Arab League Project on empowering Arab Youth, she is also active in several Egyptian

NGOs. A member in the Egyptian Women Writers Association, and the Egyptian Philosophical Society, she is a cofounder of the women's group at the Egyptian Society for Spiritual and Cultural Research, as well as the secretary general of ZKH Foundation. Prof. Rafea wrote many opinion pieces in Egyptian newspapers, including regularly for *Nahdet Misr*. In 2002 Prof. Rafea was a visiting professor at Randolph-Macon Woman's College, where she lectured on "Islam in the modern world" and "The universal meaning of the Egyptian civilization." Professor Rafea is a fellow of the Society for Applied Anthropology (SFA), a member at the American Anthropological Association (AAA), the American Sociological Association (ASA), and the International Leadership Association (ILA). She was awarded a certificate of recognition from The Egyptian Human Rights Organization. She joined the Global Peace Initiative of Women in 2011 and was invited to attend several meetings arranged by GPIW. www.hfegypt.org · www.esscr.org

The DNA of Our SOUL Cannot Be Genetically Modified!
Swami Omkarananda
Swami Omkarananda is the Spiritual Director of the Sivananda Yoga Vedanta Center in Los Angeles. Originally from Australia, she moved to the UK over forty years ago as a newly qualified doctor and worked as a psychiatrist in the NHS. Eighteen years later, she became involved in yoga, gave up paid work, and moved to live in an urban ashram in UK. She joined the International Sivananda organization in 2004 and moved to California, where she managed the Grass Valley ashram for three years. She moved to Los Angeles in 2008 and became a Swami in 2011. She is passionate about building interfaith community, networking, Vedanta, Vedic ecology, permaculture, and helping people to develop spiritually.
www.sivananda.org/la

The Power and Importance of the Seed:
The Heritage of Nature's Intelligence
Acharya David Frawley (Vamadeva Shastri)
David Frawley is a recognized Acharya and Pandit, a master teacher of Vedic knowledge in India, where he is also known as Vamadeva Shastri. He is the author of over thirty books on Yogic and Vedic subjects published in twenty different languages over the last thirty years. He is an Ayurvedic doctor and senior teacher, with a special

concern for ecology and protecting the Earth. He is the Director of the American Institute of Vedic Studies, a Master Educator for Chopra Center University, a special advisor for Kerala Ayurveda Academy, and one of the four main founding advisors for the National Ayurvedic Medical Association USA (NAMA).
www.vedanet.com

The Interbreath of Life and the Seeds It Scatters 'Round Our Planet
Rabbi Arthur Waskow

Rabbi Arthur Waskow, Ph.D., founded and directs The Shalom Center. He has pioneered the development of Eco-Judaism through the Green Menorah organizing project of The Shalom Center and the Interfaith Freedom Seder for the Earth, as well as through such books as *Trees, Earth, & Torah: A Tu B'Shvat Anthology*; and *Torah of the Earth: 4,000 Years of Ecology in Jewish Thought*. He also wrote "Jewish Environmental Ethics: Adam and Adamah," in the *Oxford Handbook of Jewish Ethics and Morality* (Elliot N. Dorff and Jonathan K. Crane, eds.; Oxford University Press, 2013). He was a founding member (2010–2013) of the stewardship committee of the Green Hevra (a network of Jewish environmental organizations), and is a member of the coordinating committee of Interfaith Moral Action on Climate.
www.theshalomcenter.org

The Rejuvenating Power of Seeds
Chief Tamale Bwoya

As Mugema (grand chief) of the Buganda Kingdom in Uganda, Tamale is trained in indigenous herbal medicine preparation and formulation. In the early 2000s he co-founded the International Institute of Traditional and Complementary Medicine in Uganda and a branch of PROMETRA in Uganda, a non-profit organization that promotes the preservation of traditional medicines and indigenous herbal knowledge in Africa. As an authority on native healing practices, Chief Tamale has attended several international and local conferences on herbal medicine, as well as participated in seminal negotiations between the Uganda government, indigenous healers, and health practitioners on traditional medicine legislation.
www.spiritualecology.org/contributor/chief-tamale-bwoya-uganda

Our Great Little Relatives—Seeds!
Rev. Doju Dinajara Freire

Rev. Doju Dinajara Freire is a Zen Buddhist nun, dancer, educator, and author. She was born in Brazil, where her affinity for expressing herself through movement was recognized early. By the age of seventeen, she was dancing and teaching professionally. Soon after her professional launch, she moved to Italy and immersed herself in the study of natural movement, children's expression, creativity, and healing. In her twenties, she added Tai Chi and Buddhism to her studies. She was ordained as a Buddhist nun in 1998 and is a disciple of Rev. Yuno R. Rech. Her educational programs on sitting meditation and a "Place for Silence" are being used in many Italian schools. Rev. Doju teaches meditation at Dojo Zen Sanrin community in Fossano. Rev. Freire has been the European representative for the Global Peace Initiative of Women helping to organize programs related to the sacred feminine and interfaith. She also conducts workshops around Italy on the unique ways of connecting with the inner silence and the healing of emotions, through dance, sacred art, meditation, and in-depth reflections.
www.youtube.com/watch?v=de1kAQ6Il54

The Seed and the Tao
Nan Lu, OMD

Nan Lu, OMD, is a Taoist master who has the unique gift of cross-cultural communication and the ability to interpret essential, timeless spiritual and healing truths with clarity, depth, compassion, and humor. He is a high-level Qigong master and a longtime doctor of traditional Chinese medicine (TCM). Dr. Lu founded the not-for-profit educational foundation, Traditional Chinese Medicine World Foundation, to bring the body–mind–spirit healing gifts of TCM to the West. He serves as a clinical associate professor at the State University of New York at Stony Brook. In his private practice at the Tao of Healing, patients experience profound shifts in body, mind, and spirit healing as do students of his Wu Ming Qigong School. Dr. Lu is passionate about helping individuals understand the profound impact of consciousness on true healing through Taoist philosophy, Chinese medicine modalities, and modern science. He lectures extensively and teaches advanced energy training classes, including LifeForce: Tao of Medical Qigong.
www.taoofhealing.com · www.tcmworld.org
www.breastcancer.com · www.tcmconference.org

The Parable of the Sower
Rev. Richard Cizik

Richard Cizik is the President of the New Evangelical Partnership for the Common Good and a leader of the "new evangelical" movement in America. This movement is committed to the principles of love not anger; a broad not narrow agenda of public concerns; unity not division; and a faith that doesn't sublimate itself to political ideology. Richard was for twenty-eight years a top government affairs leader of the National Association of Evangelicals until he was forced out of his role due to standing on principle for the reality of climate change and the importance of "creation care." He is an ordained minister, speaker, activist, writer, and public intellectual for a new kind of religious leadership that cares for the Earth.
www.newevangelicalpartnership.org

The Secret of the Seed
Sraddhalu Ranade

Sraddhalu Ranade is a scientist, educator, and one of the leading scholars on the teachings of the late Indian sage, Sri Aurobindo. He has lived for all of his life at the Sri Aurobindo Ashram in Pondicherry and studied under the tutelage of M.P. Pandit, one of the close disciples of Sri Aurobindo and the Mother. He leads retreats, delivers talks, and conducts workshops on a range of themes, including Vedic philosophy, ecology and worldview, integral education, self-development, Indian culture, science and spirituality, spiritual evolution, and yoga. Over the years he has addressed many thousands of students on these topics from numerous schools, colleges, and universities all over India and has conducted numerous intensive teacher-training workshops in integral and value-based education.

Seeds Are the Transcendent Stuff of Life
Blu Greenberg

Author and lecturer Blu Greenberg has published widely on contemporary issues of feminism, Orthodoxy, and the Jewish family. Among her many public roles, she chaired the first and second International Conferences on Feminism and Orthodoxy in 1997 and 1998 and is founding president of JOFA, the Jewish Orthodox Feminist Alliance. She is author of *On Women and Judaism: A View from Tradition*; *How to Run a Traditional Jewish Household*; *Black Bread, Poems after the Holocaust*, and others. Dialogue has also been a long and steady passion of hers. Active in ecumenical circles, Blu was a founding member of Women of Faith (Jewish-Christian-Muslim trialogue, 1980–92) and co-founder of The Dialogue Project (Jewish and Palestinian women, 1989–94). She has been a participant in many interfaith and inter-ethnic enterprises, including the Jewish Tibetan Encounter in Dharamsala (1990) and several consultations of the World Council of Churches. She was a founding member and co-chair of the Global Peace Initiative of Women (GPIW) and helped chair the Women's Partnership for Peace in the Middle East gathering at the Nobel Peace Institute in Oslo that convened more than 100 Israeli and Palestinian women for dialogue. She is married to Rabbi Irving Greenberg with whom she shares five children and twenty-three grandchildren.

The Stunted Seed
Teny Pirri-Simonian

Teny Pirri-Simonian, an adult educator, lay theologian, and researcher in the Sociology of Religions, is a member of the Armenian Orthodox Church, Catholicosate of Cilicia, Antelias, Lebanon. She grew up in the Middle East and is currently living and working in Switzerland. She has held leadership positions in the Middle East Council of Churches (MECC) and the World Council of Churches (WCC), paying special attention to women in the Orthodox Churches. Currently she is the Representative for Ecumenical and Interfaith Relations for Europe of her Church, a member of the Central Committee of the World Council of Churches, and a member of the Commission on Churches and Religions of the Council of Churches in the Canton of Vaud (Switzerland), co-founder of the European Project for Interreligious Learning (EPIL), and lecturer in Religion and Ethics at Webster University Geneva Campus. She has written extensively on the role of women in the church and society, and on women living together in religiously pluralist societies. She is an advisor to the Global Peace Initiative of Women. www.epil.ch

The Seed-ing of Consciousness, Seed-ing of the Heart
Tiokasin Ghosthorse

Tiokasin Ghosthorse is a member of the Cheyenne River Lakota Nation of South Dakota, and has a long history with Indigenous activism and advocacy. He is a survivor of the "Reign of Terror" from 1972 to 1976 on the Pine Ridge, Cheyenne River and Rosebud Lakota Reservations, and the U.S. Bureau of Indian Affairs Boarding

and Church Missionary School systems designed to "kill the Indian and save the man." An international speaker on Peace, Indigenous and Mother Earth perspectives, he recently was awarded Staten Island's Peacemaker Award for 2013. He is a returning guest faculty at Yale University's School of Divinity, Ecology and Forestry regarding the cosmology, diversity and perspectives on the relational/egalitarian vs. rational/hierarchal thinking processes of western society. Tiokasin has been the host of *First Voices Indigenous Radio* for the last 21 years (in New York and Seattle/Olympia, WA). A master musician, and a teacher of magical, ancient, and modern sounds, Tiokasin performs worldwide and has been featured at the Cathedral of Saint John the Divine, Lincoln Center, Madison Square Garden, the Metropolitan Museum of Art, and the United Nations, as well as at numerous universities and concert venues. He is a board member of several children's organizations that work to enhance living conditions and the opportunity to think culturally, spiritually, and mentally from their place of Indigeneity. He is a perfectly flawed human being and a Sundancer of the Lakota Nation.
www.firstvoicesindigenousradio.org

Seeds and the Cosmic Seeding of Oneness
Sufi Rehman Muhaiyaddeen
Sufi Rehman Muhaiyaddeen has walked through his own journey of self-realization aimed at resolving the grave dilemma of human life, which manifests as the disparities of thought and action. When he found himself incapable to resolve the dilemma of life by the apparent means, he dove deep within to eventually embrace the vision to witness the fundamental scheme of cosmic unification in all aspects of the universe, including human life. He then contributed his life for the promotion of peace and harmony in the world and looks forward to a great universal transformation of peace, unity, and trust during the coming years. In Pakistan, he is the founder and the servant at the Sufi Circle Lahore, dedicated to compose human personality through Sufi *zikr* and *muraqaba* (meditation). Moreover, he serves as the director of Green Living Association (GLA)—an organization for Environmental Peace focused on building responsible, peaceful, and globally-aligned future generations of Pakistan. GLA originated as a response to the lack of respect for Earth's biodiversity, which will inherit a vastly degraded planet if world peace does not become a reality and destruction of the natural environment continues at the present rate. Previous

to his spiritual pursuits, Sufi Rehman served Amnesty International (AI) as President of the Pakistan chapter, Member of AI's National Executive Committee, as well as Treasurer and President of Amnesty International, Lahore Group.
www.greenlivingasc.org

The Language of the Seed
Anat Vaughan-Lee

Anat Vaughan-Lee met her Sufi teacher, Irina Tweedie, in England when she was 21, and has followed the Naqshbandi Sufi path ever since. During her time in the UK, she studied with the English mystical painter and writer Cecil Collins, and taught for many years using his unique method of teaching, both in England and then in the USA, where she has lived for the past two decades. For many years she has been working with groups and dreamwork in the Sufi tradition, which encourages the deep feminine way of inner listening. In 2003 she was a delegate to the first Global Peace Initiative for Women conference at the Palais des Nations (UN) in Geneva. She also gave a presentation at "Making Way for the Feminine," a gathering of women spiritual leaders held in Jaipur, India, in 2008. Recognizing the need and urgency of the moment for the re-emergence of the feminine, she compiled and edited the writings of her husband, Sufi teacher Llewellyn Vaughan-Lee, on the subject of the sacred feminine, which has emerged as one of the rare books in this field: *The Return of the Feminine and the World Soul*. Together with her husband, she is involved in raising awareness of the deep ecological crisis of the Earth and has helped with the creation of the recent publication *Spiritual Ecology: The Cry of the Earth*, as well as its rich and informative website.
www.spiritualecology.org.

Cosmic Ecology and Diversity: Lessons from the Vedas
Swamini Svatmavidyananda

Sri Swamini Svatmavidyananda Saraswati, a longtime disciple of Paramapujya Swami Dayananda Saraswati of India, is an accomplished scholar of Vedanta. For several years, she has led an active satsang community in the United States, serving as the Spiritual Director of Swami Dayananda's USA center: Arsha Vijnana Gurukulam, based in Georgia, Washington, DC, and Oregon.
www.arshavm.org

118

PHOTO CREDITS

NAVDANYA & VANDANA SHIVA

Navdanya means "nine seeds" (symbolizing protection of biological and cultural diversity) and also the "new gift" (for seed as commons is based on the right to save and share seeds). A network of seed keepers and organic producers spread across 17 states in India, it is a women-centred movement for the protection of biological and cultural diversity.

NAVDANYA Office
A-60, Hauz Khas
New Delhi · 110 016 · India
www.navdanya.org

GLOBAL PEACE INITIATIVE OF WOMEN

The Global Peace Initiative of Women (GPIW) is an interreligious organization that seeks to bring spiritual resources to aid in addressing critical global issues. The basis of their work is the dynamic expression of unity, emerging from the heart of wisdom of the world's spiritual traditions, and our own hearts, into a new story for the human community. An essential part of this shift is the coming into a sacred relationship with the Earth and all the living forces of the universe. Feminine wisdom and the power of love can serve as the fulcrum for this inner and outer transformation.

GLOBAL PEACE INITIATIVE OF WOMEN
301 East 57th Street, 4th Floor
New York · NY · 10022 · USA
www.gpiw.org

THE GOLDEN SUFI CENTER is a California religious nonprofit 501 (c) (3) corporation, which publishes books, video, and audio on Sufism, mysticism, and spiritual ecology.

THE GOLDEN SUFI CENTER
P.O. Box 456 · Point Reyes Station · CA · 94956-0456 ·USA
tel: 415-663-0100 · fax: 415-663-0103
www.goldensufi.org · www.spiritualecology.org